The ♠
Bridge ♥
Player's ♦
Bible ♣

The
Bridge
Player's
Bible

Julian Pottage

BARRON'S

A QUARTO BOOK

First edition for the United States,
its territories and dependencies,
and Canada published in 2006 by
Barron's Educational Series, Inc.

*All inquiries should be addressed
to:*
Barron's Educational Series, Inc.
250 Wireless Boulevard
Hauppauge, New York 11788
www.barronseduc.com

ISBN-13: 978-0-7641-5900-8
ISBN-10: 0-7641-5900-3

Library of Congress Control No.
2005920485

QUAR.TBBI

Conceived, designed, and
produced by
Quarto Publishing plc
The Old Brewery
6 Blundell Street
London N7 9BH

Senior Editor Jo Fisher
Art Editor Claire van Rhyn
Designer Jill Mumford
Assistant Art Director Penny Cobb
Picture Researcher Claudia Tate
Text Editor Tracie Davis
Proofreader Natasha Reed
Photographer Martin Norris
Indexer Pamela Ellis

Art Director Moira Clinch
Publisher Paul Carslake

Manufactured by Modern Age
Repro House Ltd, Hong Kong
Printed by Midas Printing
International Ltd, China

9 8 7 6 5 4 3 2 1

CONTENTS

Introduction	6
Getting Started	10

Bidding
Opening Bids	22
Responses	35
Rebids and Continuations	51
Slam Bidding	69
Other Systems	75
Overcalls	79
Takeout Doubles	96
Penalty Doubles	10(
Competitive Decisions	11:

The Play

Opening Leads	120
Suit Combinations	137
General Play Techniques	150
Play at No-trump Contracts	168
Play at Suit Contracts	176
Endgame Strategy	194
Defender's Following Suit	214
Defensive Leads and Switches	230
Defender's Discards and Ruffs	240

Glossary	250
Index	252
What To Do Next and Further Reading	255
Useful Web Sites and Credits	256

Introduction

BRIDGE IS A GAME for four players, with two partnerships in competition with each other. The game is played with a standard pack of 52 playing cards and each deal comprises two phases: the bidding, and the play. During bidding, the two sides compete to determine the trump suit (if any) and the number of tricks they expect to make. The last bid is the contract. The play is similar to any whist-type game, with tricks won by high cards and trumps. If the contract is made, the side that bid it will get a score. If not, the other side gets a score.

The partnership element in bridge is what sets it apart from other well-known mind games such as chess, poker, and backgammon. The social element brings many friendships and often a partnership at the bridge table becomes one at home or vice versa. Bridge combines the cut and thrust of an auction (as you have in poker) with the beauty and juxtaposition of moves (as in chess) with the element of luck you have in backgammon and blackjack. While it is common for bridge players to play chess or backgammon as well, it is very rare for them to abandon bridge in favor of another game. Often they have tried the other game first and found it not quite satisfying. Another measure of the game's strength is the fact that in 99 percent of bridge games little or no money changes hands. The game has such an inherent appeal that there is no need to add a financial element to make it interesting.

One of the beauties of bridge is that you can learn the basics of the game in a few hours while it takes a lifetime to master. Even world champions will come across situations or opponents that they have not encountered before. This makes it almost impossible for anyone to become bored by the game.

After a period when longer working hours and the introduction of competing attractions (such as computer games) put the game in decline, it has enjoyed a revival in recent years, no doubt helped by the fact that people are living longer and so have more leisure time. My own club (Basingstoke at the time of writing) has seen its attendance grow so much that it is considering an extension to its premises.

Bridge is a game that you can play whether you are nine (that was how old I was when I first learned) or 90. You can play a game whether you are a carpenter, a cab driver, a physician, or a CEO. You can play the game whether you are able-bodied or no longer so mobile—with Braille cards, you can even play if you are blind. You can play the game socially with your friends or a little more seriously at a club—and there are plenty of national and international tournaments for the enthusiast. With the advent of online clubs, it is no longer a problem if you live in an isolated location or your other commitments limit the time you can devote to the game.

Bridge engenders partnership, teamwork, communication, and attention to detail—many of the attributes an employer might look for. Studies have shown that keeping one's mind active may help to preserve brain cells and delay the onset of Alzheimer's disease. Bridge offers you the chance to take your mind off whatever life may throw at you and is a lifeline to many people who otherwise have few social contacts.

The game's stars have come from all over the globe—I could fill the page with them if space permitted. Top Americans include Ely Culbertson, Charles Goren, Bobby Hamman, and Bobby Wolff. From Europe, we have Giorgio Belladonna (Italy), Paul Chemla (France), Geir Helgemo (Norway), and Terence Reese (England). From South America we have Gabriel Chagas (Brazil), from Asia we have Zia Mahmood (Pakistan), and from Australasia, Ron Klinger (Australia).

Plenty of players would be famous even if they did not play bridge. These include Bill Gates (Microsoft Chairman), Warren Buffett (investment manager), Dwight Eisenhower (U.S. president), Martina Navratilova (tennis ace), Omar Sharif (film star), Robert (Lord) Winston (gynecologist), Iain Macleod (U.K. Chancellor of the Exchequer), Somerset Maugham (writer), and the modern game's inventor, Harold Vanderbilt (yachtsman).

Omar Sharif is just one of a list of famous bridge players.

Julian Pottage

Chapter One
Getting Started

What you need and the rank of cards

FOR A GAME OF BRIDGE, you need four players, a table, and at least one pack of cards. Usually people play for at least four deals or a complete rubber, which takes half an hour or so. Many people prefer to spend an entire afternoon or evening and play several rubbers. Ideally, the table should be square with a green baize covering, and be either indoors or protected from the sun, rain, and wind outside. It is also possible to use informal surroundings, such as a train car.

The four players form two partnerships (like doubles at tennis) in competition with each other. You sit facing your partner and at right-angles to your two opponents. In bridge literature, it is customary to refer to the players by compass positions, with North and South as partners for one side and East and West as partners for the other side. You can form the partnerships either by agreement or by cutting. To cut for partners, spread a pack of cards face down on the table and each draw a card.

Whoever draws the highest card plays with the player who draws the second highest, and the players with the two lowest cards play together. The player who draws the highest card is dealer for the first deal. To determine the highest card, the cards take the same rank as they do in the play (see page 12) with the ace highest and the two lowest. If two (or more) cards are of equal rank, the suit counts, with spades highest and clubs lowest just as in the bidding.

Most players sort their cards into suits, with red and black suits alternating.

For the very first deal, the player to the left of the dealer shuffles the cards. The dealer then moves the cards to his or her right and the player on the dealer's right cuts the cards. (From here on, when using a pronoun, certain players—opener, overcaller, North, and East—are designated male, and certain players—responder, advancer, South, and West—are female.) The dealer then distributes the cards, clockwise, face down and one at a time to the four players, starting with the partner of the player who cut the cards. If two packs are in use (the norm), the second pack should have a different color or design from the first pack. The dealer's partner then shuffles this pack while the deal is taking place and puts the cards on his or her right for use on the second deal (the dealer rotates clockwise).

At the end of the deal, the players pick up their own cards and hold them in a fan and in such a way that no other player can see the faces of their cards. It is customary (and 99.9 percent of players do this) to arrange the cards into suits and order within suits. In each suit, the ace (if you have it) is high and so at the left and the two (if you have it) is at the right. It is normal to alternate red and black suits.

The bidding (see pages 12–13) will then take place followed by the play (see page 14). At the end of the play, the players will count the number of tricks won by each side to determine whether or not the contract is made and the number of any overtricks or undertricks. They will then record the score (see page 15) on a scorecard or piece of paper. Once this process is complete, a new deal begins. The player who had been to the left of the first dealer is the dealer this time. Once the rubber (see page 15) or agreed number of deals (normally four, hence the name "four-deal" bridge) is complete, the players will add up the scores and, if there is a stake, settle up. (It is usual to round to the nearest 100. Stakes are typically agreed as so many cents a point.) If the game is to continue, the players will, if they cut for partners initially, change partners at this point.

Boards for storing deals at duplicate (see page 17).

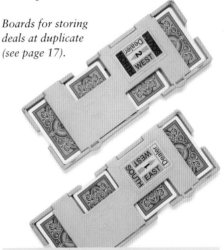

IMPORTANT POINT
A different method of dealing (for use by explicit agreement only) is a goulash. In this case, the cards from the previous deal or pass-out are not shuffled. They are then dealt in groups of three or four cards at a time to the players. The effect is to produce wild distributions.

The bidding process

THE GENERAL OBJECTIVE in bridge is to bid and make a contract. A bid comprises two components: a number and a denomination.

Let us consider the numbers first. Each player starts with 13 cards and the play produces 13 tricks (you play one card to each trick). There are no kudos for making less than half the tricks, so the first six tricks are ignored in bidding numbers. A bid of one is therefore an undertaking to take seven tricks, a bid of two to make eight tricks, and so on up to a bid of seven to make all 13 tricks. The denomination can be any of the four suits—spades, hearts, diamonds, and clubs—or a fifth strain, "no trumps." The denomination of the final bid determines the trump suit, if any. Therefore, a bid of 1♥ literally means, "I undertake to make seven tricks with hearts as trumps." (In the early rounds of

bidding, you bid more to describe your hand than because you expect your bid to end the auction. The common bidding system in North America is Standard American, in which a major-suit opening promises five cards and a 1NT opening is strong.) If you make a bid in "no-trumps" (some writers omit the hyphen and/or use the singular), you are saying that you do not want there to be a trump suit. A bid of "Three No-trumps" literally means, "I undertake to make nine tricks with no suit as trumps."

Bids only increase and the strains rank in the order "no-trumps" (highest), spades, hearts, diamonds, and clubs. The lowest bid is thus 1♣ and the highest is Seven No-Trumps (7NT). If someone else has bid,

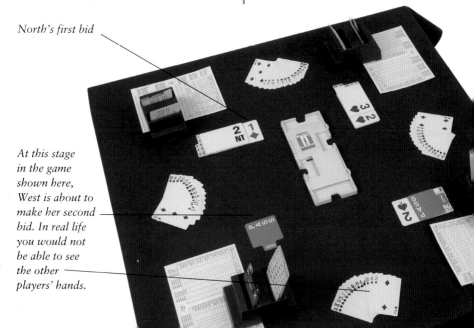

North's first bid

At this stage in the game shown here, West is about to make her second bid. In real life you would not be able to see the other players' hands.

Sample auction:

SOUTH	WEST	NORTH	EAST
PASS	PASS	1 ♣	1 ♥
1 ♠	3 ♥	4 ♠	5 ♥
PASS	PASS	DOUBLE	PASS
PASS	PASS		

Bidding box commonly used at duplicate.

you can bid at the same level in a higher strain or at a higher level in any strain. If the previous bid is 2♥, you can therefore bid 2♠ or 2NT. If you wish to bid a minor suit (clubs or diamonds), you must do so at the three level or higher. There is no requirement to bid at the minimum level. You can bid higher if you wish; indeed, it would be quite common to jump if partner bids a suit that you like very much. If you do not wish to make a bid, you say "pass" (in certain countries, including the U.K., "no bid" is used instead of "pass"). When someone has bid and three players in a row pass, the bidding ends.

Apart from the 35 possible bids and "pass," there are two special calls: double and redouble. A double has the effect of increasing the trick score if the contract makes and the penalty if the contract fails. A redouble has the effect of increasing the trick score and penalty still further. You can double only an opposing bid and you can redouble only if an opponent has doubled. A double literally means, "I do not think you can make your contract."

In the unusual event that all four players pass (a pass-out), the cards are shuffled and the dealer rotates as usual.

NOTE

❏ South and West did not have a good enough hand to start the bidding and so passed. Note that West raised her partner's hearts with a jump, and that North raised his partner's spades, again with a jump. To double, North must think that 5♥ will go down (in other words that East–West cannot make 11 tricks, so North–South can take at least three). The auction ends with three passes and 5♥ doubled becomes the final contract. (Since all auctions end with three passes, elsewhere the abbreviation "End" is used to denote the three final passes.)

❏ In making your bids (and passes) you should try to maintain an even tone in your voice. It is contrary to the rules and spirit of the game to place deliberate emphasis on a bid or part of a bid.

IMPORTANT POINT
At duplicate (see page 17), players usually bid using bidding boxes rather than their voices. You place the bid on the table in front of you so that all the other players can see it.

The play process

AT THE END of the bidding, one player becomes declarer and assumes responsibility for his cards as well as those of his partner (known as dummy). Declarer is the first member of the partnership that buys the contract to have bid the strain in which the contract is. (For example, if South responds 1♥, she will be declarer in any North–South heart contract.)

The player on declarer's left makes the opening lead, placing a card on the table so that the other players can see it. For all other tricks, the player who won the previous trick leads (plays first to) the trick.

After the opening lead, dummy displays his hand, arranging the suits in columns with the trumps (if any) on his right. His duty is simply to comply with declarer's instructions about what cards to play. On any lead, the other players have a duty, if they can, to follow suit, in other words, play a card of the suit led. If you have no cards in the suit led, you can play any card. Similarly, when on lead, you can play any card.

The card that wins the trick is, when there are no trumps on the trick, the highest card in the suit led. On any trick containing a trump, the highest trump wins the trick. Suppose these are the cards played:
♣2 [Led] by East—wins if clubs or spades are trumps or there are no trumps
♥7 by South—never wins
♥8 by West—wins if hearts are trumps
♦A by North—wins if diamonds are trumps.

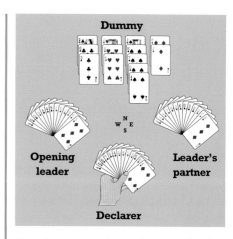

Dummy

Opening leader

Leader's partner

Declarer

One player on each side keeps a pile of the tricks won by the side and arranges them so that the number of tricks in each pile is clear (see diagram below). By the end of the play, there will be 13 tricks in all and from this it will be clear whether the contract was successful.

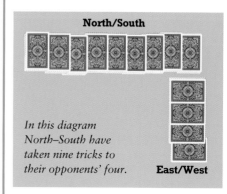

North/South

In this diagram North–South have taken nine tricks to their opponents' four.

East/West

Scoring (see right) takes place at the end of the play. If, in this example, the contract is at the three-level or lower, the contract has made. The score (in rubber bridge) will then be below the line.

Scoring at rubber bridge

TRICK SCORES * (BELOW THE LINE)

Score for each trick over six bid and made	Not doubled	Doubled	Redoubled
Minor suit trumps	20	40	80
Major suit trumps	30	60	120
No-trumps first trick	40	80	160
No-trumps further tricks	30	60	120

OVERTRICK AND UNDERTRICK SCORES

	Not Vulnerable			Vulnerable		
	Not dbld.	Dbld.	Redbld.	Not dbld.	Dbld.	Redbld.
For each overtrick	Trick score	100	200	Trick score	200	400
For 1 undertrick	50	100	200	100	200	400
2 undertricks	100	300	600	200	500	1000
3 undertricks	150	500	1000	300	800	1600
4 undertricks	200	800	1600	400	1100	2200
Each further undertrick	50	300	600	100	300	600

SLAM BONUSES

Small slam (12 tricks) bid and made	500 (nonvul)	750 (vul)
Grand slam (13 tricks) bid and made	1000 (nonvul)	1500 (vul)

BONUSES FOR HONORS

Four trump honors (A, K, Q, J) in one hand	100
Five trump honors (A, K, Q, J, 10) in one hand	150
Four aces in one hand at no-trumps	150

BONUSES FOR DOUBLED CONTRACTS

Any doubled contract made	50
Any redoubled contract made	100

BONUSES AT END OF A RUBBER *

For winning a rubber if opponents have won no game	700
For winning a rubber if opponents have won a game	500
For winning the only game in an unfinished rubber	300
For having the only part-score in an unfinished game	100

* Two games win a rubber; a trick score of 100 or more is game; for game in a single deal, you need to make 3NT, 4♥/♠, 5♣/♦, or, if doubled, 2NT, 2♥/♠, 3♣/♦ or, if redoubled, 1NT/♥/♠ or 2♣/♦.

Scoring at duplicate and in four-deal bridge

Trick scores: the same as at rubber bridge

Overtrick and undertrick scores: the same as at rubber bridge

Bonus for making a nonvulnerable game: 300

Bonus for making a vulnerable game: 500

Bonus for making a part-score (duplicate only): 50

Bonus for a part-score on the fourth deal at four-deal bridge: 100 (Note: Some people play that part-scores do not carry forward at four-deal bridge, in which case part-score bonuses are the same as those at duplicate.)

Honors: count at four-deal bridge but not at duplicate

SCALE OF INTERNATIONAL MATCH POINTS

For most teams-of-four matches

Swing	IMPs	Swing	IMPs
0–10	0	750–990	13
20–40	1	1000–1090	14
50–80	2	1100–1290	15
90–120	3	1300–1490	16
130–160	4	1500–1740	17
170–210	5	1750–1990	18
220–260	6	2000–2240	19
270–310	7	2250–2490	20
320–360	8	2500–2990	21
370–420	9	3000–3490	22
430–490	10	3500–3990	23
500–590	11	4000+	24
600–740	12		

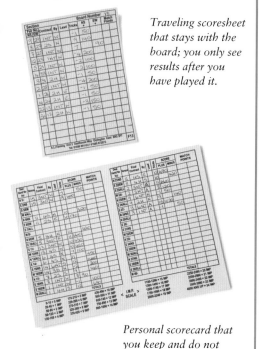

Traveling scoresheet that stays with the board; you only see results after you have played it.

Personal scorecard that you keep and do not show to opponents.

Example: Team A score 620 at one table (4♥ made vulnerable) and lose 170 at the other (3♥ with an overtrick). They gain a swing of 450 (620–170), which equates to 10 IMPs. If the score at the second table were 790 (4♥ doubled made), they would lose a swing of 170 (790–620) and 5 IMPs.

IMPORTANT POINT

Board-a-match (also known as point-a-board) is a simpler method for comparing scores at teams. You record a win, a loss, or a tie depending on which team has the higher score.

Duplicate and four-deal bridge (Chicago)

DUPLICATE IS THE NORM in competition play. So that you can play the same cards as at other tables and compare scores, you store played cards differently. Instead of putting your card in the middle of the table, put it down in front of you so that the other players can see it. (In duplicate, the opening lead is initially made face down. This gives the leader's partner the chance to ask questions about the meaning of any opposing bids, except at this point, you may ask only about opposing bids or plays when it is your turn to bid or play.) When the trick ends, turn the card over, placing its short side toward your partner if you won the trick or the long side if you lost it. You place played cards in order and partly covering one another.

At any point in the play and at its conclusion it is therefore clear how many tricks each side has won. At the end of each deal, you return the cards to the wallet or board from which you drew your cards.

In duplicate, the markings on the board or wallet determine which side(s) are vulnerable and who is the "dealer" (who bids first). (It is slightly different in four-deal bridge. Neither side is vulnerable on the first deal, both sides are on the fourth deal, while the sides take turns on the second and third. The dealer rotates as in rubber bridge.)

Most clubs and many tournaments compare scores with matchpoints. You will be given 1 matchpoint for each score you beat and 0.5 for each with which you tie (or, according to local custom, 2 and 1 respectively). For example, suppose a "board" has been played seven times. If you are -100 and the other scores are +140, -100, -300, -500, -620, and -620, you get 0.5 for tying with -100 and 4 for beating the four larger minuses. This gives you 4.5 matchpoints out of 6 (or 9/12).

In this example, your side has won the first three tricks, lost the next two, won the two after that, and lost the eighth trick:

Point count

TO VALUE HOW MUCH their hand is worth (and hence how much to bid with it) players the world over use a method called point count.

Ace =
4 points

King =
3 points

Queen =
2 points

Jack =
1 point

There are thus 40 points in a pack
(10 points in each of four suits) and an average hand contains 10 points.

Players make slight adjustments for unsupported honors or good spot cards. In addition, as you may already know, long suits and short suits can help your hand's trick-taking potential, especially in a suit contract. The simple adjustment for distribution is as follows:

Doubleton = 1 point
Singleton = 2 points
Void = 3 points

You should not count a short suit in partner's main suit as an asset and you do not count short suits as assets for a no-trump bid. If your side has a good trump fit (at least nine cards between the two hands in the proposed trump suit), a more accurate valuation (sometimes called "dummy points") is as follows:

Doubleton = 1 point
Singleton = 3 points
Void = 5 points

In this book, if high card points (HCPs) are referred to, this means points for high cards only. When, as will be the norm, points are simply referred to, it means HCPs plus distribution points as appropriate.

Points are useful in judging how high to bid. In general, the partnership needs the following points for the contracts stated:

1NT or 2 of a suit	20-22
2NT or 3 of a suit	23-24
3NT (game)	25-27
4NT	28-30
5NT	31-32
6NT (small slam)	33-36
7NT (grand slam)	37-40
4 of a major (game)	26-28
5 of a minor (game)	29-31

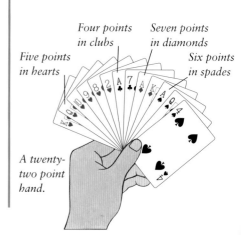

Four points in clubs

Seven points in diamonds

Five points in hearts

Six points in spades

A twenty-two point hand.

Other valuation methods

LOSING TRICK COUNT—applies only when you have a fit.
Count at most three losers in a suit and deduct losers for aces, kings, and normally, queens.

No loser suits: Void, A alone, A–K alone, A–K–Q to any length
One loser suits: Singleton K or lower, K–x or A–x, A–K–x, A–Q–x, K–Q–x
Two loser suits: Q–x or worse, A–x–x, K–x–x, Q–J–x

Count Q–x–x as three losers unless you have an ace elsewhere or partner has bid the suit.

Typical loser counts

Game forcing opening = three or fewer losers
Strong two opening (if not game forcing) = four losers
Strong one-level opening or typical jump shift response = five losers
Good one-level opening or minimum jump shift response = six losers
Minimum opening or game values as responder = seven losers
Two-level response or invitational jump raise of an opening = eight losers
One-level response or single raise of an opening = nine losers

To work out how many tricks the partnership can make, add your losers to partner's losers and deduct the answer from 24. So, if you have a spade fit and both have seven-loser hands, you can probably make game in spades (24–7–7=10)

Quick tricks (defensive tricks)—likely to score whatever trumps are:
A–K = 2 QT, A–Q = 1.5 QT, A or K–Q = 1 QT, K= 0.5 QT.
For a game-forcing opening you want 5QT. For a marginal one-level opening, you might add the number of cards in your two longest suits to your HCP and your quick tricks. If the total is 22 or more, you open.

Playing tricks—tricks with your long suit as trumps:
Count 0.5 of a trick for any four-card suit and one trick for each card over five. Then add high card tricks. These are A–K–Q = 3, A–K–J = 2.5, A–Q–J or K–Q–J = 2, A–Q or K–Q–10 = 1.5, A, K–J–x or Q–J–x = 1, etc.

One loser in hearts

One loser in clubs

No losers in diamonds

One loser in spades

A twenty-two point hand and three losers.

Chapter Two
Bidding

OPENING BIDS

Strength required

To open the bidding at the one level, you should have a minimum of 13 points, at least 10 of which should be high card points (HCP). Here you have 11 points in high cards and, counting 1 point for each doubleton, 13 in total. You can open 1♠ and expect to rebid 2♠ over a response of 1NT or two of a suit.

YOU	PARTNER
1♠	

The upper limit for opening at the one level is about 21 points. Here you have 19 points in high cards and, counting 2 for the singleton, a total of 21. After opening 1♣, you intend to make a strong rebid; most likely 2♥.

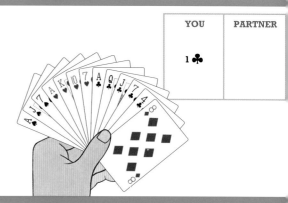

YOU	PARTNER
1♣	

This hand is similar to the first, but with the ♣A changed to the king. The point count has now fallen to 12 and you have only one defensive trick (each king counts as a half). Partner tends to expect one-and-a-half or two defensive tricks for an opening one bid, confirming that this hand is too weak.

YOU	PARTNER
PASS	

IMPORTANT POINT *Since you generally need 26 points to make game, it is important that you or your partner find a bid when* *holding 13 points. If not, you might pass out a deal on which you have game.*

Opening bids of one of a suit

When you have enough to open, you normally open with one of your longest suit. In modern methods, an opening of 1♥ or 1♠ promises five cards or more in the suit opened. With this hand, 1♥ is the correct opening.

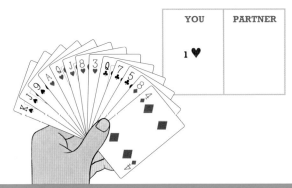

YOU	PARTNER
1♥	

When you open one of a minor, especially clubs, you quite often have only a three-card suit. This hand, with 19 points, is too strong for 1NT and not quite strong enough to open 2NT. So the opening is 1♣.

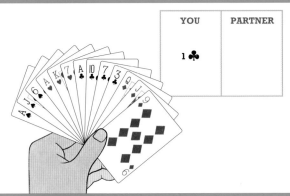

YOU	PARTNER
1♣	

There is no official upper limit for the number of cards in the suit opened. In practice, because hands with an eight-card suit are rare, seven cards is the normal maximum. Here you have 13 points, good intermediates in diamonds—the 10–9—and two defensive tricks. Open 1♦.

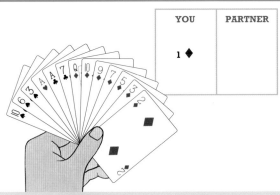

YOU	PARTNER
1♦	

IMPORTANT POINT *An opening bid of one of a suit covers such a wide range that it is normal to call it "unlimited." In fact, the upper limit is about 21 points. If you have more, you might miss game if partner cannot respond.*

Opening with two-suited hands

If you have a five-card suit and a four-card suit, you invariably open the five-card suit. A bid in a suit suggests to partner that you might like to have the suit as trumps, and you want to have as many trumps as possible. Anyway, you could not contemplate a 1♠ opening on this hand because you have only four spades.

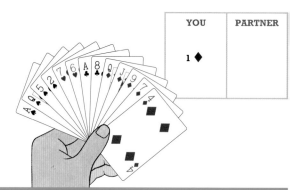

YOU	PARTNER
1♦	

With touching suits of equal length, you open the higher ranking no matter what. If you open 1♥ and rebid 2♦, partner will have the chance to put you back to your first suit at the two level. The same could not be said if you wrongly opened 1♦.

YOU	PARTNER
1♥	

With non-touching suits, typically spades and diamonds or hearts and clubs, again the rule is to open the higher suit. If you open 1♥ and partner responds 1NT or 1♠, you will have the chance to rebid 2♣. With five–five in the black suits, some open 1♣, but this is only advisable if the spades are poor.

YOU	PARTNER
1♥	

IMPORTANT POINT *When you open one of a suit, you need to think of your rebids over any likely response. On occasion, you might open your second longest suit; for example, if you are 1–5–6–1 with only 13–15 points.*

Opening with three-suited hands

A hand containing three suits of at least four cards in length is known as three-suited. Where one of the suits is five cards in length, you open in that suit. True, if the five-card suit ranks immediately above your void suit, it may not be easy to show your other suits. Even so, it is best not to distort the relative lengths of the suits.

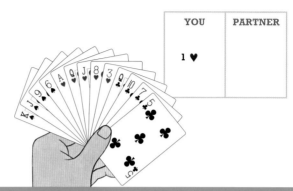

YOU	PARTNER
1 ♥	

With three four-card suits and a singleton, the traditional rule was to open the suit below the singleton whenever possible. On this hand, some open 1 ♦ knowing they can rebid 1 ♠ over 1 ♥. The modern approach is to open 1 ♣, which makes it easier to find a club fit. You can still rebid 1 ♠ over 1 ♥.

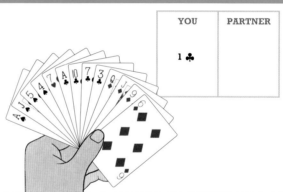

YOU	PARTNER
1 ♣	

Since you do not open four-card majors, you have no choice but to open your minor. This allows partner to respond in either major at the one level. If partner responds 2 ♣, a 2NT rebid will be correct despite the singleton.

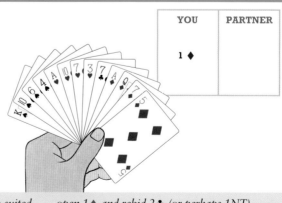

YOU	PARTNER
1 ♦	

IMPORTANT POINT *Awkward three-suited hands include 0–4–4–5 and 1–4–4–4. With the former, open 1 ♣. With the latter, open 1 ♦ and rebid 2 ♣ (or perhaps 1NT) over 1 ♠.*

Opening with balanced hands

With a balanced hand (no singleton and at most one doubleton), you try to open 1NT if you are in the right range. These days the usual range for 1NT is 15–17. So, with 16 HCP, this hand is perfect. If you play the old-fashioned 16–18, 1NT would also be fine. If you open 1♦, you will have no good rebid.

YOU	PARTNER
1 NT	

This hand has 13 HCP and is not good enough for a strong no-trump opening. Instead you open 1♣. If partner responds 1♠, you will rebid 1NT, which will then show 12–14.

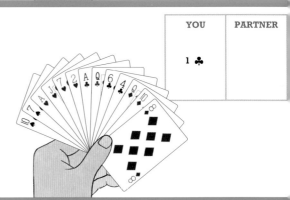

YOU	PARTNER
1 ♣	

With 18 HCP, you are too good for 1NT if the range is 15–17. Since you do not have a five-card major, you open 1♦. This makes it easy to find a four-four fit in either major, because partner will show a four-card major in preference to raising diamonds.

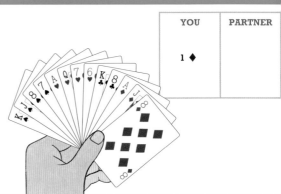

YOU	PARTNER
1 ♦	

IMPORTANT POINT *A 1NT opening describes both the distribution and the strength of your hand. It often leaves partner in a better position to decide how high to go and which suit, if any, to play in.*

Two club openings and continuations

If your hand is so strong that you can envision game facing a near Yarborough, you open an artificial, forcing 2♣. Ideally, you have five or more defensive tricks and at least 22 points. The bid says nothing about your clubs (you might be void) and partner must (with one exception) keep the bidding open until you reach game.

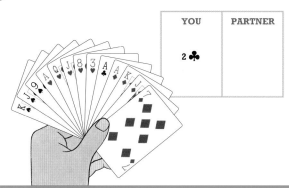

YOU	PARTNER
2♣	

With 23 or more HCP, you open 2♣ even on a balanced hand. You intend to rebid 2NT showing these values (23–24 HCP). If the initial response is a negative (2♦ for most but 2♥ for some tournament players), your 2NT rebid can be passed.

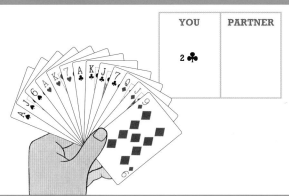

YOU	PARTNER
2♣	

2♦ on the first round is just keeping the bidding open. On the next round, you cannot support hearts (you would need three or more hearts to raise), so you show your club suit. Even if partner does not like clubs, it may be helpful to know your holding because this may make it possible to play in 3NT.

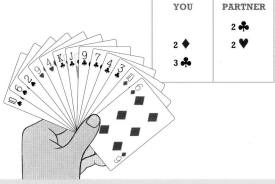

YOU	PARTNER
	2♣
2♦	2♥
3♣	

IMPORTANT POINT *An opening of 2♣ creates a forcing situation, enabling you and your partner to find a fit at a low level. This helps you to reach the best game and possibly look for a slam.*

2NT opening and continuations

**A common range for a 2NT
opening** is 20–22 HCP. Some
prefer 20–21 and a few still play
22–24. Check with your partner
what range you are playing. With
so much strength, it is unlikely
that you have a suit unstopped.
If you did, it would not be too
much cause for concern; nor
should a five-card major.

YOU	PARTNER
2 NT	

With a balanced hand, you can
raise a 20–22 2NT to 3NT with
at least 5 points. You can invite
with 4NT if your side might have
33 points, raise to 6NT if you can
count 33–34 points, and raise to
7NT if you can count 37 points.

YOU	PARTNER
	2 NT
3 NT	

With an unbalanced hand and
a five-card (or longer) major,
you can bid three of a major.
This asks partner to raise (or cue
bid) with three-card or better
support for your suit and
otherwise to bid 3NT. Indeed,
apart from the absence of a weak
takeout, responses are very
similar to those to a 1NT
opening. See pages 45–49.

YOU	PARTNER
	2 NT
3 ♥	

IMPORTANT POINT *A 2NT opening
describes the shape and the strength of your
hand well and will help partner to judge the*
*best contract. Opening 2NT is also likely to
protect tenaces in your hand.*

Strong two openings and continuations

Traditionally, two-level openings are natural and forcing to game. For a strong two, you need at least nine tricks in your hand; this hand is fine. If, instead, you play weak twos, open 1♠.

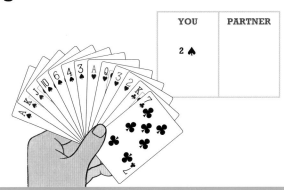

YOU	PARTNER
2 ♠	

One advantage of the strong two is that partner, with a weak hand, must keep the bidding open with a 2NT negative. This enables you to show your second suit on the next round if you have a two-suited hand. Partner can then express preference between the suits.

YOU	PARTNER
2 ♠	2 NT
3 ♥	

You need an ace and a king (or the equivalent) to give a positive response, so keep the bidding open with a 2NT negative. Partner's rebid guarantees at least six spades so, with tolerance for spades, you raise to game.

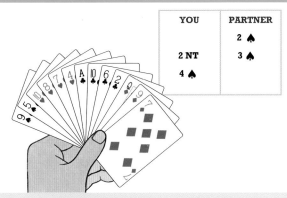

YOU	PARTNER
	2 ♠
2 NT	3 ♠
4 ♠	

IMPORTANT POINT *Strong two openings are on the wane even among social players because you can open an artificial 2♣ and show your suit on the next round.*

Weak twos

A weak two opening shows a hand with a six-card suit too weak for a one-level opening. A typical range is 6–10 (or 5–9) HCP. The idea is to make life hard for the opponents while describing your hand to partner. You should have some values in your suit because partner may either lead it or sacrifice in it.

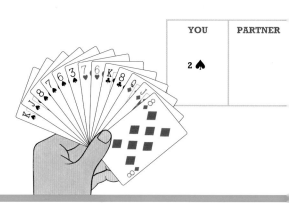

YOU	PARTNER
2 ♠	

Even when vulnerable, this hand is fine for a weak opening of 2♥. The hand will play so much better if hearts are trumps than if they are not. The singleton and doubleton increase your playing strength, and it is very unlikely that your side belongs in clubs.

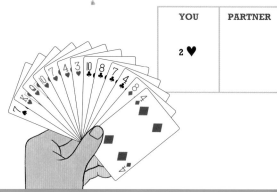

YOU	PARTNER
2 ♥	

Some play weak twos in the majors only. Others play them in diamonds as well. Even so, this hand is ill-suited. First, with four good spades, you may miss a spade contract if you open 2♦. Second, bidding such a weak suit may cause partner to go astray either in the bidding or on the opening lead.

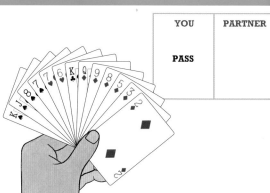

YOU	PARTNER
PASS	

IMPORTANT POINT *Many tournament players use weak twos. They have good preemptive effect by themselves, and partner, with support, can often raise to make the opponents' life even harder.*

Three-level preempts

An opening three bid is like a weak two, but with even more shape and playing strength. In case someone doubles, you want to be within about two tricks of your bid when you are vulnerable and within about three tricks if you are non-vulnerable. This hand is worth 6–7 tricks and is fine for 3♥ at any vulnerability.

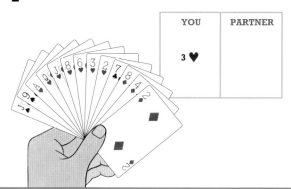

YOU	PARTNER
3 ♥	

This hand has less shape (no singleton) and an inferior suit (one of the top two honors rather than two). It will still be worth 3♠ if you are non-vulnerable. Vulnerable, a pass is more prudent, or you could open 2♠ if that is weak in your system.

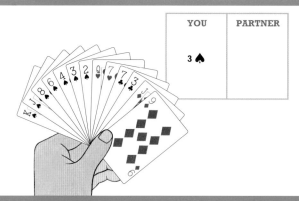

YOU	PARTNER
3 ♠	

You have an opening bid yourself, it is true, but you must pass if partner opens 3♥. To bid 3NT would be foolish—partner's hand may well be useless to you. 4♥ might make if partner has good hearts and is short in diamonds, but the odds are against it.

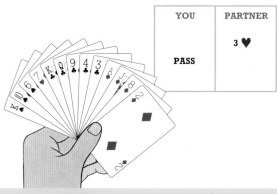

YOU	PARTNER
	3 ♥
PASS	

IMPORTANT POINT *A preemptive opening is usually single suited and, as responder, you will usually either pass or raise. To bid on (other than raising to add to the pre-empt) you need values similar to a strong no-trump opener.*

Four- and five-level openings

In first or second seat, openings at the four level are like those at the three level but with more shape. You will often have an eight-card suit or a seven-card suit with two singletons. Again, the rule is that you should be roughly within two tricks of your bid if vulnerable or within three tricks if you are non-vulnerable.

YOU	PARTNER
4 ♠	

If you open four of a minor, you rule out playing in 3NT. This means that, facing an unpassed partner, you have added reason to wait for a hand with a lot of shape. Here the desire to stop the opponents from finding a major-suit fit justifies the bid.

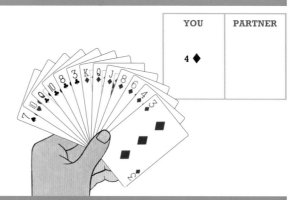

YOU	PARTNER
4 ♦	

An opening of five of a minor is still preemptive and is quite likely to buy the contract. You need to have eight or nine tricks in your hand. As with all the preemptive openings, you will normally have less than 10 HCP.

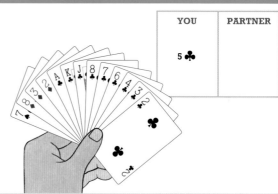

YOU	PARTNER
5 ♣	

IMPORTANT POINT In third seat, when partner's initial pass will often enable you to tell whether your side can have a game or slam on, you can afford to vary your preempts.

Gambling 3NT

If you have a very strong balanced hand, you can start with 2♣. This leaves a 3NT opening free for a different type of hand—one with a solid minor. The most common treatment is that you deny an outside ace or king. For 3NT to make, partner will need a stopper of sorts in the other three suits and at least one card in your presumed suit.

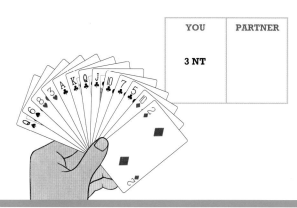

YOU	PARTNER
3 NT	

Clearly partner's solid minor is clubs and, with hopes of stopping the other three suits, you pass. Facing the example opening hand, you will make seven club tricks, the ♦A, and one other trick—in hearts if the defenders do not get busy in the other suits.

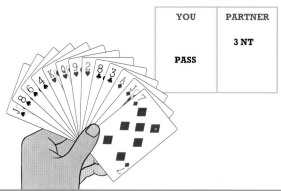

YOU	PARTNER
	3 NT
PASS	

Now you have nothing in hearts and it is prudent to retreat. You bid 4♣ because partner presumably has a solid suit of clubs. This is a "pass or correct" bid. With running diamonds, partner would bid 4♦ over 4♣.

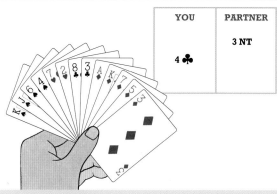

YOU	PARTNER
	3 NT
4 ♣	

IMPORTANT POINT *It will come up less, but you can play 3NT as showing a running suit and side stoppers. This avoids playing 3NT from the wrong side. Partner will either pass or make a slam try.*

4NT Opening

A 4NT OPENING ASKS FOR SPECIFIC ACES	
The responses are as follows:	
5♣	NO ACES
5♦	ACE OF DIAMONDS
5♥	ACE OF HEARTS
5♠	ACE OF SPADES
5NT	TWO ACES
6♣	ACE OF CLUBS

You could open 2♣ intending to go to at least a small slam in diamonds. However, it may be hard to find out whether partner has the useful ♠A or the useless ♥A. After opening 4NT, you will bid the small slam if partner shows no aces or the ♥A. You will bid the grand slam facing the ♠A and 7NT facing two aces.

YOU	PARTNER
4 NT	

Again, the 4NT opening should simplify the auction and make it difficult for the opponents to compete. You will pass 5♣ or 6♣, bid 6♣ over 5♥, and bid 7NT if partner shows two aces by bidding 5NT.

YOU	PARTNER
4 NT	

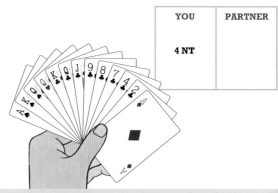

IMPORTANT POINT *Before opening 4NT, make sure you can cope with all the possible responses and that it will tell you what you need to know.*

RESPONSES

Supporting a major

With 6 points or more, you respond to a one-level opening bid. If it is a major, your first priority is to decide whether you can raise partner's suit. Four-card support is always good enough for a raise. The upper limit for a single raise is a poor 10 points.

YOU	PARTNER
	1♠
2♠	

With three-card support for a major and a ruffing value, it is still correct to give a single raise. To bid 1NT or 2♣ with this hand would be a mistake. If your side belongs in 3NT, you can still get there because a rebid of 2NT or 3NT by opener is natural.

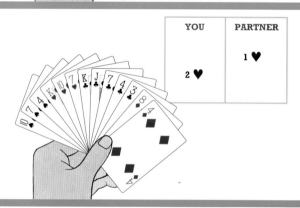

YOU	PARTNER
	1♥
2♥	

Since an opening in a major promises a five-card suit, you raise even with a 4–3–3–3 hand. Establishing a fit is always a priority. You would also raise 1♥ to 2♥. Responding 1NT would be misleading. Partner would assume that you hold a doubleton at most in the suit opened.

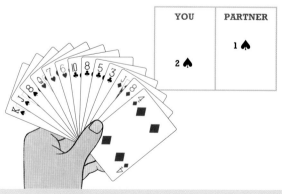

YOU	PARTNER
	1♠
2♠	

IMPORTANT POINT *Since the most common game is four of a major, it is important to establish whether you have* *a major-suit fit. Also, if the opponents come in, knowing that you have a fit helps you compete.*

Flexibility over a minor

To make game in a minor you need 11 tricks. This means that, even if your side has a four-four fit in a minor, it may be better to play in a major-suit or no-trump contract. To show a four-card major is especially important because (a) partner cannot open a four-card major and (b) one of a minor may be on a three-card suit.

YOU	PARTNER
	1 ♦
1 ♥	

Five-card support suffices to raise a minor, even if partner has only a three-card suit. Nevertheless, it is still better to show a major if you sensibly can. Although a no-trump contract looks unlikely with this hand, you could well belong in spades if partner has support.

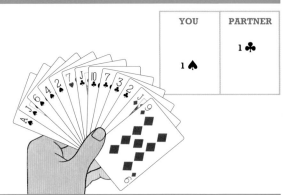

YOU	PARTNER
	1 ♣
1 ♠	

With such a terrible heart suit, common sense tells you to support diamonds. You do not want a heart lead or partner to raise on three to an honor. Even more, you do not want LHO to have room to overcall in spades at the one level.

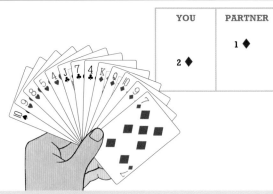

YOU	PARTNER
	1 ♦
2 ♦	

IMPORTANT POINT *Note the important difference between responding to major- and minor-suit openings. A change of suit normally denies support for a major but not necessarily for a minor.*

Jump raises

Since a single raise normally shows 6–10 points, with a better hand you must do something else. The modern treatment is that a jump raise invites game and is not forcing. It shows 11–12 points. Here you have 9 HCP and 1 point for each doubleton.

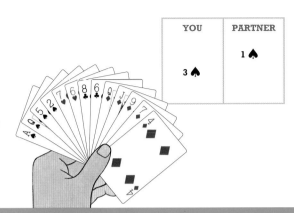

YOU	PARTNER
	1 ♠
3 ♠	

Four-card support for a minor is not enough for a jump raise. You need five cards to give jump support of a minor when the opener may have only three cards. Note that you should not jump raise a major with three-card support.

YOU	PARTNER
	1 ♦
3 ♦	

With five-card support for partner's major and good shape, you need fewer values to raise to game. Indeed, many pairs play that you have to find some other bid if you have more than 10 HCP. With the two five-card suits, this hand is too strong to bid only 3 ♥. In any case, you want to shut the opponents out if you can.

YOU	PARTNER
	1 ♥
4 ♥	

IMPORTANT POINT *Many tournament players play "inverted raises" of minor-suit openings. A single raise is then forcing, suggesting 11+ points, while a jump raise is preemptive.*

Strong raises

This hand, with a singleton and 13 points in high cards, is too good for either 3♠ or 4♠. If you do not have a conventional way to show the hand, you start with a forcing bid in a new suit and support partner strongly on the next round. This is called a delayed game raise.

YOU	PARTNER
	1 ♠
2 ♥	

Many duplicate players play a convention known as a splinter. This shows a singleton or void in the suit bid, at least four-card support for partner, and the values to raise to game. In this context, the bid of 4♥ is a perfect description of this hand.

YOU	PARTNER
	1 ♠
4 ♥	

Many duplicate players play another convention, a Jacoby raise. In this, a bid of 2NT promises four-card or better support for partner's major and a minimum of 11 HCP and 13 total points. Opener's rebid then describes his shape and you can start investigating slam possibilities at a low level.

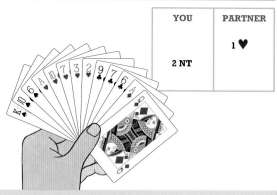

YOU	PARTNER
	1 ♥
2 NT	

IMPORTANT POINT *If you have opening bid values and support for opener's major, you can be sure of game and will often have a slam. This is another reason why agreeing the suit is so important.*

1NT response

If you do not have support for partner and cannot show a suit of your own at the one level, you will often find yourself responding 1NT. The range for this is about 6–10 HCP. With a weaker hand you pass, while with a stronger hand you can show a suit at the two level.

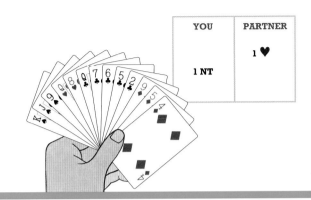

YOU	PARTNER
	1 ♥
1 NT	

If partner opens a major, especially spades, you may have to respond 1NT on an unbalanced hand. Perhaps partner will bid some other suit at his next turn. Because your bid is limited, opener can pass a 1NT response in standard methods.

YOU	PARTNER
	1 ♠
1 NT	

If partner opens a minor, especially clubs, a 1NT response is likely to indicate a balanced hand—you would show a four-card major rather than bid 1NT, and sometimes it will be right to bid a four-card minor. Here, in any event, the flat shape and scattered values suggest a 1NT response. 1NT over 1♣ suggests 8–10 HCP.

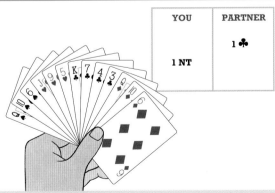

YOU	PARTNER
	1 ♣
1 NT	

IMPORTANT POINT *Some play that a 1NT response to a major is semi-forcing. Opener has to bid again except with a 5–3–3–2 type and 12–14 HCP.*

One-level suit responses

With 6 points and length in a suit higher ranking than partner's, you can bid a suit at the one level in response to an opening. Unless you have previously passed, a change of suit response is forcing—opener has to bid again.

YOU	PARTNER
	1 ♥
1 ♠	

There is no upper limit to the strength for bidding a new suit at the one level. Here you have 17 HCP. With a hand this strong, you naturally bid your longest suit first. Remember, partner must bid again, so you will have the chance to show both your strength and other features of the hand later.

YOU	PARTNER
	1 ♣
1 ♦	

With four cards in each major, you bid 1♥. This leaves partner room to support hearts or rebid 1♠ and so makes it easy to find a four-four fit in either major. If you bid 1♠, partner may not be strong enough to rebid 2♥, which would be a reverse. You might then miss a four–four heart fit.

YOU	PARTNER
	1 ♣
1 ♥	

IMPORTANT POINT *When playing five-card majors, it is more important to show a four-card major than a longer diamond suit.* *So, if you have no more than 10 points, you respond in the major.*

Two-level suit responses

You need at least 11 points to respond at the two level. If you are responding in a minor, a four-card suit will suffice. With this hand, you can respond 2♣.

YOU	PARTNER
	1 ♠
2 ♣	

To respond at the two level in a major (the only sequence for this in an uncontested auction being 1♠–2♥), you promise a five-card suit. You promise to bid again over any normal opener's rebid; the same applies if you respond in a minor.

YOU	PARTNER
	1 ♠
2 ♥	

Since you do not respond at the two level in a four-card major, 2♦ is the correct bid, not 2♥. If partner holds four hearts, he can rebid 2♥. Even if you play five-card majors, do not jump raise with only three-card support, so 3♠ here would be wrong. You can support spades later.

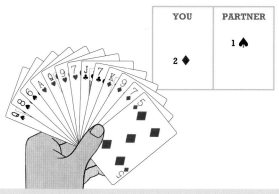

YOU	PARTNER
	1 ♠
2 ♦	

IMPORTANT POINT *If you respond at the two level, you promise to bid again even if opener merely rebids his suit at the two level or raises your suit to the three level.*

Choice of responses

In the modern style, a responder's reverse (2♦ now and 2♠ next time) is a game force. Here, with 11 HCP, you have the values to invite game rather than force to it. So you respond 1♠, not 2♦.

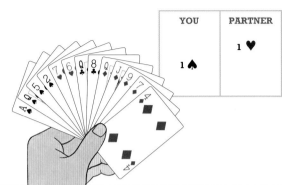

YOU	PARTNER
	1♥
1♠	

This time, with your suits touching, you can show both suits without promising a great deal of strength. You respond 1♠ and intend to rebid 2♥ if partner's rebid is a 12–14 1NT or 2♣.

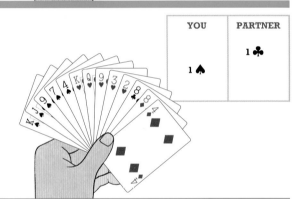

YOU	PARTNER
	1♣
1♠	

With two four-card suits you tend to bid suits up the line, but common sense dictates an exception here. With concentrated values in diamonds, you bid your stronger suit rather than the cheaper suit. This way partner will value a singleton club as an asset. A response of 2♣ would be misleading.

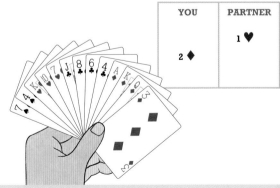

YOU	PARTNER
	1♥
2♦	

IMPORTANT POINT *As responder, you need to consider opener's likely rebids and what further action, if any, you intend to make.* *Doing this should help you to decide on the correct initial response.*

Jump shifts

A jump in a new suit after partner opens is called a jump shift. It is forcing to game and indicates 16 points upward. By creating a game force at once, you allow both you and your partner to bid naturally and find the best fit. With this hand, you intend to rebid your spades to show a suit needing very little support.

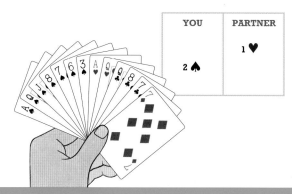

YOU	PARTNER
	1 ♥
2 ♠	

Another hand type for a jump shift is one with support for partner and a good suit of your own. In this case, you intend to bid clubs next. With a two-suited hand, you only make a jump shift if partner opens one of your two long suits. Note that if you passed as dealer, then a jump shift promises a fit and a hand just short of opening values.

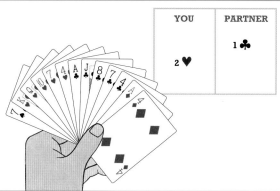

YOU	PARTNER
	1 ♣
2 ♥	

With all suits stopped, you can also make a jump shift on a semi-balanced hand. You make a jump bid in your five- or six-card at your first turn and rebid 2NT (if sufficient) or 3NT. Partner will expect 16–19 points for this sequence.

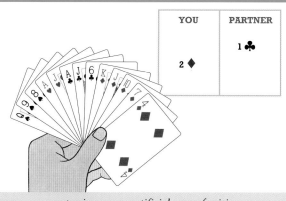

YOU	PARTNER
	1 ♣
2 ♦	

IMPORTANT POINT *Some players have abandoned strong jump shifts. They either play that jumps are weak, like a weak two opening, or an artificial way of raising opener's suit ("Bergen" raises).*

2NT and 3NT responses

Traditionally, a jump response to 2NT shows 13–15 and is forcing to game. You promise a stopper or two in each of the unbid suits. Also, you should not have a four-card major that you could show at the one level.

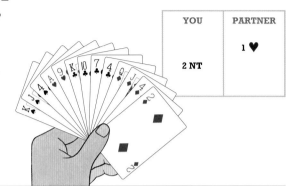

YOU	PARTNER
	1 ♥
2 NT	

If 2NT shows 13–15, a 3NT response shows 16–18 points. It is not forcing, but opener will be aware of the values you are showing and may look for a slam with extras.

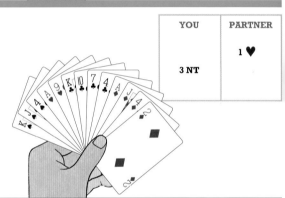

YOU	PARTNER
	1 ♥
3 NT	

Here you are too weak for either 2NT or 3NT and so respond in your cheapest four-card suit. You might bid 2NT on the next round. If you had already passed, you could bid 2NT immediately, when the range would be 11–12.

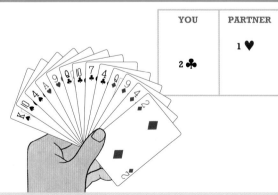

YOU	PARTNER
	1 ♥
2 ♣	

IMPORTANT POINT Some duplicate players do not play either 2NT or 3NT as natural. Instead, they play that the response agrees the suit opened and is forcing to game (see page 38).

Balanced hands after 1NT

With a balanced hand (and no
five-card major), you pass if there
is no hope of 25 HCP in the two
hands. When there might be 25
HCP, if partner is maximum,
you raise to 2NT. Facing a 15–17
1NT opening, you are thus worth
an invitational raise to 2NT.

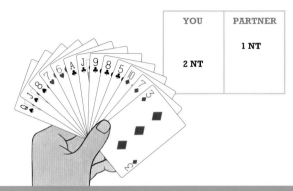

YOU	PARTNER
	1 NT
2 NT	

With a balanced hand, you can
jump to 3NT if you can count
25 HCP (or more) for the
partnership. Responding to a
15–17 1NT, this will be the case.

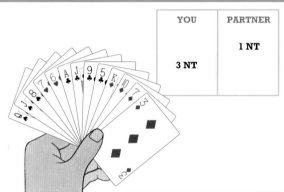

YOU	PARTNER
	1 NT
3 NT	

Facing a 15–17 1NT, there is a
chance your side has 33 HCP. To
invite a slam, raise to 4NT. This
is a non-forcing quantitative bid.
As a direct raise, it does not ask
for aces.

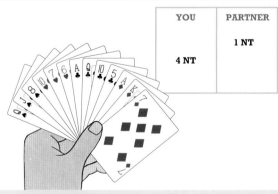

YOU	PARTNER
	1 NT
4 NT	

IMPORTANT POINT *With enough points to
count 33–34 for the partnership, raise to*
6NT. If these will only be present if partner is
maximum, make an invitational raise to 4NT.

Weak takeout after 1NT

With a weak hand and a long suit facing a 1NT opening, it is likely that the hand will play better in a suit. With spades as trumps, your hand might be worth four tricks. It may be useless in 1NT. A bid of a suit (other than clubs) at the two level shows a weak hand and asks partner to pass.

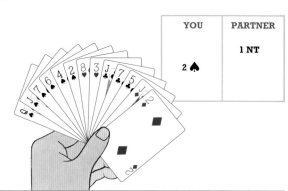

YOU	PARTNER
	1 NT
2 ♠	

A six-card suit is the ideal, but it is usually right to make a weak takeout with a five-card major or with five diamonds and not a 5–3–3–2 shape. Unless partner has the ♥A, this hand may be nearly useless in 1NT. It might be worth four tricks with hearts as trumps.

YOU	PARTNER
	1 NT
2 ♥	

The poor diamond suit coupled with the values in the short suits makes passing 1NT the correct action. If the range is 15–17, you expect partner to make seven tricks without necessarily setting up the diamonds. Even if 1NT fails, you cannot be sure that anything else is better.

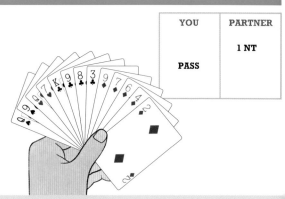

YOU	PARTNER
	1 NT
PASS	

IMPORTANT POINT *Few duplicate players use weak takeouts. They play "transfers," by which you bid the suit below the one in which you have length. See page 49 for details.*

Stronger hands after 1NT

A jump to three of a suit in response to 1NT is forcing to game and indicates 10+ HCP facing a strong no-trump. With three- or four-card support, opener raises or makes a cue bid. Without it, he bids 3NT. If you have a six-card major, you can jump straight to game over 1NT, assured of an eight-card fit.

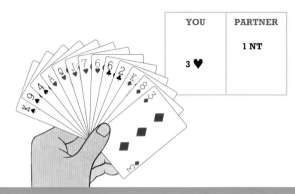

YOU	PARTNER
	1 NT
3 ♥	

A jump to three of a minor suggests either an unbalanced hand, like this one, or slam interest (which you also have facing a strong 1NT). If opener bids a new suit at the three level, this initially shows strength (a stopper) in the suit.

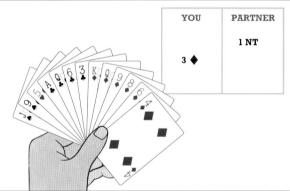

YOU	PARTNER
	1 NT
3 ♦	

With game values, a balanced type, and length in a minor, you do not bother to show the minor. It is too unlikely that you can make five of a minor but not 3NT. Just raise to 3NT.

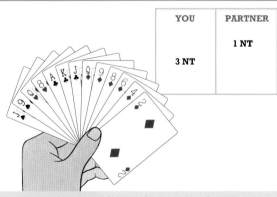

YOU	PARTNER
	1 NT
3 NT	

IMPORTANT POINT *Since a 1NT opening shows a balanced hand, you can rely on partner to have at least two cards in any suit you might bid.*

Stayman over 1NT

You have the values to raise a strong no-trump to game. It might be better, however, to play in a four-four major fit. Your artificial 2♣ asks opener to bid 2♥ with four hearts, 2♠ with four spades, and 2♦ with no four-card major. You intend to raise to 3NT if opener does not show a four-card major.

YOU	PARTNER
	1 NT
2 ♣	

Playing a strong no-trump, you have enough to invite game. The way to do this is to start with Stayman. If opener bids 2♦, you rebid 2♥. Opener can then pass if minimum, jump to 4♥ or 3NT if maximum, or bid 3♥ or 2NT on an in-between hand.

YOU	PARTNER
	1 NT
2 ♣	

Normally, you must have length in one or both majors to use Stayman. The one exception is when you hold a string of clubs. 2♣ followed by 3♣ is the traditional way to escape into clubs.

YOU	PARTNER
	1 NT
2 ♣	2 ANY
3 ♣	

IMPORTANT POINT *With a weak three-suited hand short in clubs—ideally 4–4–5–0—you can use Stayman and pass any opener's rebid. This is very likely to leave you in a better contract than 1NT.*

Transfers after 1NT

Most duplicate players use transfers over 1NT, bidding 2♦ to show hearts and 2♥ to show spades. This will make the 1NT bidder declarer and helps responder describe her hand. Here you will rebid 3NT over opener's normal 2♥ rebid. Opener then chooses whether or not to play in hearts.

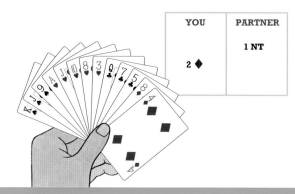

YOU	PARTNER
	1 NT
2 ♦	

After making a transfer and hearing partner complete it, you may be able to show a new suit. This is best played as forcing to game. Remember, your 2♦ showed hearts, so 3♦ was the first time you showed diamonds.

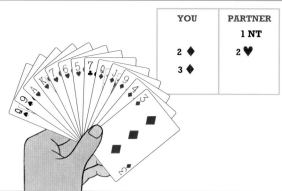

YOU	PARTNER
	1 NT
2 ♦	2 ♥
3 ♦	

Now you have a weak hand, but the transfer still works well. Partner must have a better hand than you and may have tenace holdings in one or more suits. The loss of the ability to make a weak takeout into diamonds is a small price to pay for using transfers.

YOU	PARTNER
	1 NT
2 ♥	2 ♠
PASS	

IMPORTANT POINT *The usual method, if you play four-suit transfers, is that a response of 2♠ shows clubs while 2NT shows diamonds.*

Responding as a passed hand

Since your initial pass means you cannot have enough to be sure of game, partner is at liberty to pass your response. This makes it much more descriptive to show both your near opening strength and balanced shape with 2NT than just to show hearts with 1♥.

YOU	PARTNER
PASS	1 ♦
2 NT	

This time your initial pass works to your advantage. You would be too weak for responding 2♥ if you were an unpassed hand. Of course, now that 2♥ is not forcing, it is obviously better than bidding a catchall 1NT.

YOU	PARTNER
PASS	1 ♠
2 ♥	

Some duplicate players use a convention known as Drury when partner opens a major in third or fourth seat. With three-card or better support, responder bids an artificial 2♣. Opener then bids an artificial 2♦ with a shaded or dead minimum opening and finds some other bid with sound values (when you will reach game).

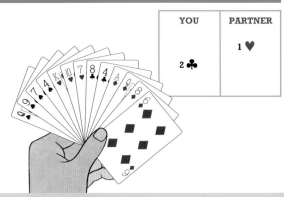

YOU	PARTNER
	1 ♥
2 ♣	

IMPORTANT POINT *When your response will not be forcing—if it will give you game (at rubber bridge with a part-score) or you have previously passed—only bid a suit if you want to play in it.*

REBIDS AND CONTINUATIONS

Supporting partner

If you open and partner responds in a suit you like, supporting it takes the same priority as it does when you are responder. Four-card support is always enough for a raise. With a minimum opening, 13–15 points, a single raise is sufficient.

YOU	PARTNER
1 ♣	1 ♠
2 ♠	

Sometimes you should raise with only three-card support. Here you have three good hearts and a ruffing value. Rebidding these moderate clubs is nowhere near as attractive, while a reverse of 2♦ would be unthinkable on a minimum opening.

YOU	PARTNER
1 ♣	1 ♥
2 ♥	

Since you told partner about your spades with your first bid, you show support for her diamonds at your second. The fact that it is a minor makes no difference in whether or not you raise the suit. Partner will not pass your raise because she has promised to bid again.

YOU	PARTNER
1 ♠	2 ♦
3 ♦	

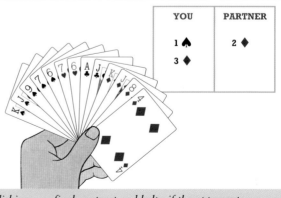

IMPORTANT POINT *As well as establishing a fit, raising partner's suit usually limits your hand. This often makes it easy to judge the final contract and helps if the opponents compete.*

Jump raises

Since a single raise shows a minimum hand, with a mid-range opening, 16–18 points, you make a jump raise. With rare exceptions, you will always have four-card support for a jump raise. Partner will bid on unless hers was a minimum response.

YOU	PARTNER
1 ♣	1 ♥
3 ♥	

A double jump, raising a one-level response all the way to game, shows a strong opening: 19–21 points. Four-card support is essential for this. Since you have reached game, partner is free to pass. However, if she can see the possibility of 33–34 points between the hands, she can bid on looking for a slam.

YOU	PARTNER
1 ♣	1 ♥
4 ♥	

If partner responds in a minor at the two level, a jump raise is absolutely forcing. If you have a better than minimum opening and partner has enough to respond at the two level, you should have game values. Going past 3NT, you need a shapely hand. Partner may make a cue bid, check on aces, or sign off in your major.

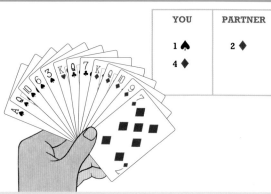

YOU	PARTNER
1 ♠	2 ♦
4 ♦	

IMPORTANT POINT *If they can, tournament players often use a conventional bid known as a splinter. It shows the same values and support as a jump raise but with a singleton or void in the suit they bid.*

Showing a second suit

Without support for partner, you usually show an unbid suit of your own if it is convenient to do so. Your rebid at the one level shows no extra values and is not forcing. If partner had responded 2♣, you would have rebid 2♦ because 2♠ would be a reverse and promise extra values.

YOU	PARTNER
1♦	1♥
1♠	

You can rebid at the two level in a suit ranking lower than your first suit without any extra values. With a weak responding hand, partner can pass 2♦ or put you back to hearts. It would be wrong for you to rebid 2♥. Partner already knows you have hearts.

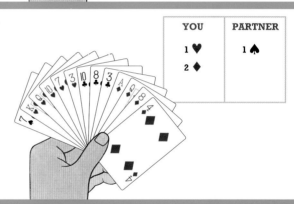

YOU	PARTNER
1♥	1♠
2♦	

Over a 1♠ or 1NT response, you would have rebid 2♣ to show your second suit. Despite your five-card club suit, you cannot do this over 2♦ because bidding at the three level shows extra values. Partner must bid again and perhaps you will be able to show your clubs next time.

YOU	PARTNER
1♥	2♦
2♥	

IMPORTANT POINT *With your rebid (indeed any bid), you look to describe new features of your hand rather than tell the same story twice. However, you cannot go above two of your first suit to show a new suit without extra values.*

Reverses and high reverses

If you open in one suit and make a simple rebid in a higher-ranking suit at the two level, this is a reverse. You promise that your first suit is longer than the second, typically with 4–5, 4–6, or 5–6 in the two suits. A reverse after a one-level response is forcing for one round and promises at least 16 points.

YOU	PARTNER
1 ♣	1 ♠
2 ♦	

A reverse after a two-level response has much the same meaning as it does after a one-level response. You promise extra values and a longer first suit than your second. The key difference is that it creates a game force rather than a one-round force.

YOU	PARTNER
1 ♥	2 ♦
2 ♠	

If you open in one suit and make non-jump rebid in a new suit at the three level after a simple response, this is a *high reverse*. You promise the same values as a simple reverse. Some players have the agreement that a high reverse promises five cards in the second suit, but the norm is that four cards are sufficient.

YOU	PARTNER
1 ♥	2 ♦
3 ♣	

IMPORTANT POINT *There is a key difference between a reverse and a high reverse. With a reverse, your first suit is longer than the second. With a high reverse, the suits may be the same length.*

Jump shift rebid

A jump in a new suit is the strongest rebid you can make and is forcing to game. You need a minimum of 19 points for the bid. You will invariably have more cards in your first suit than in your second if (as here) the first suit is lower ranking.

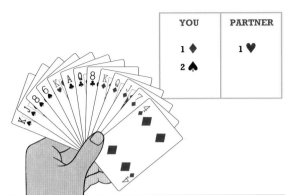

YOU	PARTNER
1 ♦	1 ♥
2 ♠	

A jump in a new suit may take you to the three level. Again, you need at least 19 points and the bid creates a game force. The slight difference is that now your second suit may or may not be the same length as your first suit.

YOU	PARTNER
1 ♥	1 ♠
3 ♣	

You can make a jump shift rebid (or reverse) after a response of 1NT. Once more, you need to have sufficient strength to force to game (19–21 points). Partner may give preference to your first suit, raise your second suit, or rebid 3NT (with stoppers in the unbid suits).

YOU	PARTNER
1 ♥	1 NT
3 ♦	

IMPORTANT POINT *Since a simple reverse is forcing, many tournament players play that a jump reverse is a splinter. It shows extra values, support, and a shortage in the suit bid.*

Giving preference

Partner has shown two suits without reversing, so you do not have to bid. With a minimum responding hand (6–10 points) and more cards in opener's second suit, you pass. 2♦ should be a much better contract than 1♥.

YOU	PARTNER
	1♥
1 NT	2♦
PASS	

Again, partner has shown two suits and may be minimum. You prefer his first suit and, to indicate game invitational values (10–12 points), you jump to 3♣. Partner, if he bids on, will often try 3NT. Some players open 1♣ and rebid 1♠ with a 4–3–3–3 shape, in which case you must be careful about raising clubs.

YOU	PARTNER
	1♣
1♥	1♠
3♣	

Although you do not much like either of partner's suits, it is still your duty to express preference between them. Since his first suit will often be longer than his second, you always go back to his first suit with equal length. To rebid 2♠ you would need much better spades while 2NT would show better values (10–12 points).

YOU	PARTNER
	1♥
1♠	2♣
2♥	

IMPORTANT POINT *You might give preference to opener's first suit with a doubleton when holding three cards in* *the second. You would certainly do this if you see a chance of game and so want to keep the bidding open.*

Other actions after opener shows two suits

Someone who opens one suit and rebids in another usually has at least nine cards between the two suits, so will often hold a singleton in your longest suit. This means you need a six-card suit, ideally with good intermediates, to rebid it. If your hand were better, say with the ♣A instead of the ♣Q, you would jump to 3♠.

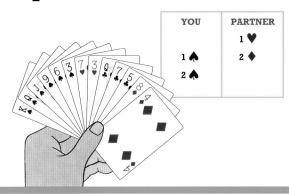

YOU	PARTNER
	1 ♥
1 ♠	2 ♦
2 ♠	

A 2NT rebid shows the same strength as an immediate limit 2NT response—a good 10 points to a moderate 12. In addition, you promise a stopper in the unbid suit and imply disinterest in opener's suits. With a good 12 points (up to about 15), you could jump to 3NT.

YOU	PARTNER
	1 ♣
1 ♥	1 ♠
2 NT	

Now you have the values to rebid 3NT, but this would be rash with no diamond stopper—the opponents may well lead the suit. The solution is to bid the fourth suit. Opener must bid again and chooses a descriptive action. This may be 2♥ with a sixth heart, 2♠ with three spades, 3♣ with a fifth club, 2NT with one diamond stopper or 3NT with two.

YOU	PARTNER
	1 ♥
1 ♠	2 ♣
2 ♦	

IMPORTANT POINT *Fourth-suit forcing is useful if you have a good hand but are unsure of the right spot; for example, after* 1♥–1♠–2♣ *the way to make a forcing club raise and stay below 3NT is to bid 2♦ and then 3♣.*

Opener's rebid in the same suit

A 1NT response is not forcing, which means that as opener you do not have to bid again. However, with an unbalanced hand, it is normal to do so. Repeating your own suit after a 1NT response (unless perhaps it is clubs) promises a six-card suit. A simple rebid shows a minimum or near minimum opening (13–16 points).

YOU	PARTNER
1 ♠	1 NT
2 ♠	

After a one-level response, a jump rebid in your suit guarantees a six-card (or longer) suit. It promises the values to invite (but not force to) game, about 16–18 points. Usually responder will either pass, raise your suit, try 3NT, or make a cue bid in support of your suit.

YOU	PARTNER
1 ♥	1 ♠
3 ♥	

After a two-level response, a jump rebid in your suit still promises a six-card (or longer) suit. Now, since it is game forcing, the range is wider, 16–21 points. After opener jump rebids in a minor, you will often end up in 3NT. This means that a new suit by responder after the jump shows a stopper in that suit.

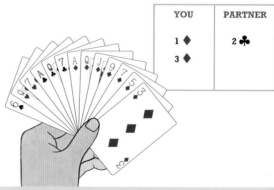

YOU	PARTNER
1 ♦	2 ♣
3 ♦	

IMPORTANT POINT *After a two-level response, a jump rebid by opener in his suit promises a solid or semi-solid suit (at most one loser). Without it, make a simple rebid in the suit as a waiting bid.*

Actions after opener rebids one suit

When opener bids a suit twice, he will certainly have at least five cards in the suit and will more often have six. So, even if it is a minor, three-card support is ample. Your simple raise is not forcing and shows the values to invite game. With no heart stopper, this is a much better bid than 2NT.

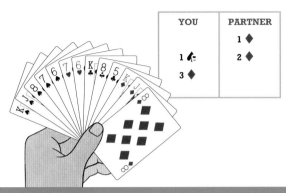

YOU	PARTNER
	1 ♦
1 ♣	2 ♦
3 ♦	

After opener rebids his suit, a new suit by responder is normally played as forcing for one round at the two level and forcing to game at the three level. You do not need to rescue partner from a suit that he has rebid. On this auction, your side could have a club fit because opener would have needed extra values to rebid 3♣.

YOU	PARTNER
	1 ♠
2 ♥	2 ♠
3 ♣	

If you do not like opener's suit, the usual rule is to stay low on a misfit. To invite game with 2NT you need 10–12 HCP and stoppers in the unbid suits. With more strength, you would jump to 3NT.

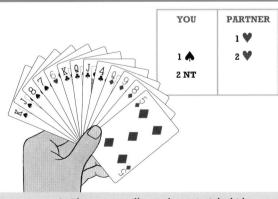

YOU	PARTNER
	1 ♥
1 ♠	2 ♥
2 NT	

IMPORTANT POINT *1. A responder's rebid in a new suit at the three level creates a game force.*

2. If you are really stuck, you might bid a three-card suit that opener is unlikely to raise (because he bypassed the suit).

Opener's 1NT rebid

Opener's 1NT rebid shows 12–14 HCP, a hand too weak to open 1NT showing 15–17 HCP. It is best to have a stopper in each of the unbid suits but, with a 4–3–3–3 shape and the appropriate point count, you rebid 1NT no matter where your values are.

YOU	PARTNER
1♣	1♥
1 NT	

See the rebid problem you have if you make the wrong opening. It would be a lie to rebid 2♦ with such a flat hand and an underbid to rebid 1NT. Some players would rebid 1♠ and take the chance that responder might raise the suit. Better still, open 1NT.

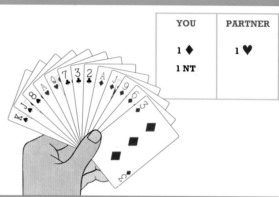

YOU	PARTNER
1♦	1♥
1 NT	

Many good players are prepared to rebid 1NT when holding a singleton in responder's suit. This avoids having to rebid a moderate suit. If you do not feel comfortable with bidding 1NT with this shape, rebid 2♣ instead.

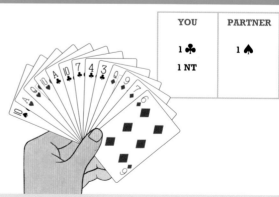

YOU	PARTNER
1♣	1♠
1 NT	

IMPORTANT POINT *When your side has bid two suits, the opponents are more likely to find your weak spot. This makes holding stoppers in the unbid suits for a 1NT rebid quite important.*

Continuations after a 1NT rebid

A 1NT rebid by partner is a limit bid and often enables you to place the final contract. With only 5 HCP, you see no hope of game and so sign off in 2♠. This should be safer than 1NT. If you had the same shape and enough to invite game, about 11 points facing 12–14, you would jump to 3♠.

YOU	PARTNER
	1 ♦
1 ♠	1 NT
2 ♠	

On a hand like this, when the early rounds of bidding show that your side does not have a fit, you are happy with a no-trump contract. As usual, raise to 3NT if you can count 25 points between the two hands, but invite with 2NT if partner would need to be maximum for this to be the case.

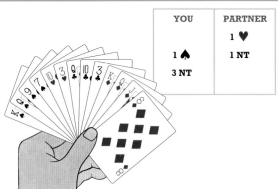

YOU	PARTNER
	1 ♥
1 ♠	1 NT
3 NT	

With an unbalanced hand, you can show a new suit at your second turn. This is forcing if it is a reverse (as here) or a jump. The spade weakness means that this hand may well play better in a suit contract.

YOU	PARTNER
	1 ♣
1 ♦	1 NT
2 ♥	

IMPORTANT POINT *Many duplicate players use some form of inquiry about opener's shape and/or range after a 1NT rebid. Names for popular versions of this are Checkback, Crowhurst, and new minor forcing.*

Opener's 2NT rebid

A jump rebid to 2NT shows a hand too good either to open or rebid 1NT; in other words 18–19 points. It normally shows a balanced hand with stoppers in both unbid suits. Although it is not forcing, partner will bid on with all but the barest minimum.

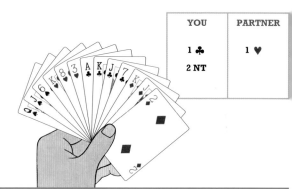

YOU	PARTNER
1 ♣	1 ♥
2 NT	

The normal range for a non-jump 2NT rebid is a good 13 or 14. With less, you do not rebid 2NT as responder, having bid at the two level, will have to bid again. Many play that you can also rebid 2NT on 15–17 in a hand ill-suited for a 1NT opening.

YOU	PARTNER
1 ♥	2 ♣
2 NT	

This sequence is fine if you have agreed that the upper limit for a non-jump 2NT rebid is 17 HCP. The weak doubleton and five-card major are reason enough not to open 1NT. Note that you would have to overbid slightly if partner responded to 1NT by raising to 2NT.

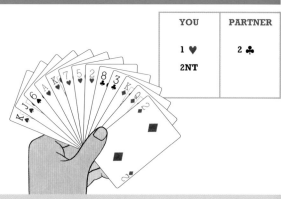

YOU	PARTNER
1 ♥	2 ♣
2NT	

IMPORTANT POINT *A 2NT rebid is unsound if you have a small doubleton in an unbid suit. It is usually better to find* *another bid, even if this means bidding a three-card suit.*

Continuations after a 2NT rebid

After opener's jump 2NT rebid, the simplest method is to play that all continuations are game forcing. 4♥ might be safer than 3NT if opener has three-card support and you give him the chance to show preference by introducing your diamonds.

	YOU	PARTNER
		1 ♣
	1 ♥	2 NT
	3 ♦	

After a non-jump 2NT rebid, it is usual to play that responder can rebid her own suit at the three level and play there. All other bids create a game force. Here, with a balanced hand yourself, you can simply raise to 3NT. Even if opener is maximum, you will not have enough for a slam.

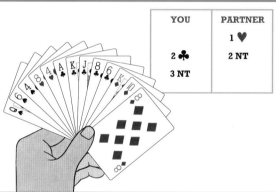

	YOU	PARTNER
		1 ♥
	2 ♣	2 NT
	3 NT	

With a highly unbalanced hand, you bid naturally, reversing with this hand to show longer clubs than hearts. A suit contract is likely to be better than 3NT. Indeed, if partner's hand fits yours well—with aces facing your singletons—there could even be a slam.

	YOU	PARTNER
		1 ♦
	2 ♣	2 NT
	3 ♥	

IMPORTANT POINT *Some tournament players use a convention, the Wolff signoff, to play in a suit part-score after opener's jump to 2NT. A bid of 3♣ requires opener to bid 3♦ and pass responder's next bid, if any.*

Opener's rebids after a raise

For game in a major, you need about 26 points between the two hands. Partner's single raise shows at most 10, so you cannot have enough (you do not count a point both for the ♣J and the doubleton club). It would be different if partner raises to 3♠. This shows 10–12, meaning you have enough values to go on to game, 4♠.

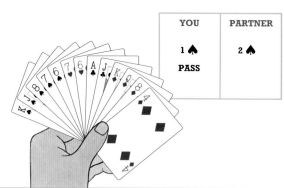

YOU	PARTNER
1 ♠	2 ♠
PASS	

With around 16–18 points, there is a chance of game, even after a single raise. To find out more about partner's hand, you make a trial bid. If you have agreed a major, the normal thing is to show a suit in which you want help. When you have agreed a minor, it is quite likely that you belong in 3NT, so you show a stopper instead.

YOU	PARTNER
1 ♣	2 ♣
2 ♦	

With 19–21 points and agreement in a major, you can go straight to game after partner's single raise. Here, because you have a known nine-card fit, you can count 3 points for the singleton spade to give you 20 points in all.

YOU	PARTNER
1 ♥	2 ♥
4 ♥	

IMPORTANT POINT *Remember that partner may have raised with three trumps. If your hand is relatively flat (e.g., a 5–3–3–2 shape), you might rebid 2NT or 3NT.*

Opener's 3NT rebid

If a jump rebid of 2NT shows 18–19 and a 2NT opening shows 20–22, you do not need a rebid of 3NT to show a strictly balanced hand. It is best to play that it shows a hand like this, with a long strong suit of your own as a source of tricks and stoppers in the unbid suits.

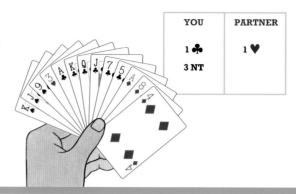

YOU	PARTNER
1♣	1♥
3 NT	

If you expect partner to hold a flat 19 (the old-fashioned meaning for some), you would remove 3NT to 4♥. In the modern style, partner will have a hand like the one above and this will not be a success. Instead, you should pass 3NT.

YOU	PARTNER
	1♣
1♥	3 NT
PASS	

Facing a hand with about 20 points, a long strong diamond suit, and control cards in the black suits, there may well be a slam on. Since you do not "rescue" a game into a part-score, 4♦ from you is forcing and sets the suit.

YOU	PARTNER
	1♦
1♥	3 NT
4♦	

IMPORTANT POINT *Some older players play that a double jump to 3NT shows 19–20 or exactly 19 balanced. Check whether your partner expects this.*

Responder's rebids after a raise

If opener raises your initial response, you have probably found the best suit in which to play and it is only a question of how high to go. The single raise shows a minimum opening, 13–15 points, so you cannot have 26 between your two hands. To go on to 4♠ you would need partner to have made a double raise (3♠).

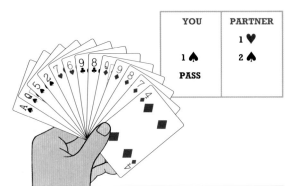

YOU	PARTNER
	1♥
1♠	2♠
PASS	

With an opening bid of your own, you knew you wanted to play in game as soon as partner opened. Having found a fit, you know what that game is and bid it.

YOU	PARTNER
	1♣
1♥	2♥
4♥	

This hand is weaker than the previous example. You do not want to be in game facing 13 points but you do facing 15. Therefore, you make a trial bid in the suit in which you want help, diamonds. Opener will look to see whether he can help you in diamonds and whether he has any extra values. He will normally either sign off in 3♥ or bid 4♥.

YOU	PARTNER
	1♣
1♥	2♥
3♦	

IMPORTANT POINT *Remember that partner may raise your major-suit response with three trumps and a ruffing value. If your response was in a four-card suit, it might be right for you to rebid 2NT or 3NT.*

Rebids after no-trump responses

You have 18 HCP and, adding at least one for the long diamonds, can be confident there will be at least 25 between the two hands. When you are happy with a no-trump contract, you raise to 3NT with 19–20, raise to 2NT with 17–18, and pass with 16 or less.

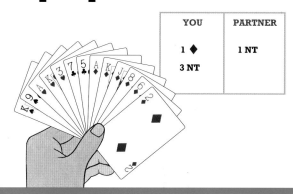

YOU	PARTNER
1 ♦	1 NT
3 NT	

Partner would have responded 1♠ rather than 1NT if she had a four-card spade suit. This means she is likely to have length in one or both minors. So, despite holding nine cards in the majors, you should pass 1NT. A 2♥ rebid would be particularly poor when your opening has already promised a five-card heart suit.

YOU	PARTNER
1 ♥	1 NT
PASS	

Even if a natural 2NT response is non-forcing (as some play it), you want to play in game with this hand. Since the club suit may be a worry in 3NT, you describe your hand further by bidding your second suit (forcing). Partner may rebid 3NT, show preference to spades, or, with strong hearts and weak clubs, bid 3♥.

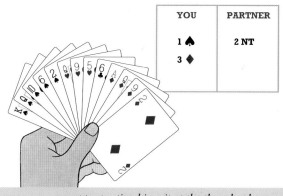

YOU	PARTNER
1 ♠	2 NT
3 ♦	

IMPORTANT POINT *After a natural non-forcing 2NT response, any rebid by opener, except repeating his suit at the three level, creates game force.*

Continuations after a no-trump response

After you have responded 1NT,
you will often pass if opener
rebids in a new suit without
reversing. This is because you
would have raised his first suit
rather than bidding 1NT if you
liked it very much. Here you do
not care much for either of his
suits but must put him back to
spades in case he is 5–4 or even
6–4 in the majors.

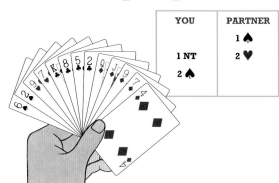

YOU	PARTNER
	1 ♠
1 NT	2 ♥
2 ♠	

If you respond 1NT and partner
rebids in a second suit, he will
often have a singleton
somewhere, usually in your
longest suit. Therefore, to bid a
new suit, you need a six-card suit
to bid it at the two level or a
seven-card suit to bid it at the
three level.

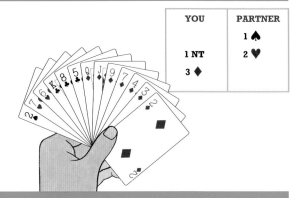

YOU	PARTNER
	1 ♠
1 NT	2 ♥
3 ♦	

When you have responded 2NT
(and hence denied a heart suit)
and partner has shown two
other suits, there is no question
of playing in hearts. Your bid of
3♥ therefore just shows strength
in the suit and, by inference,
weak spades.

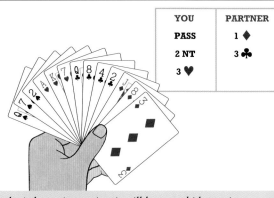

YOU	PARTNER
PASS	1 ♦
2 NT	3 ♣
3 ♥	

IMPORTANT POINT *When you have denied
a long suit, as with a 2NT or 3NT response,
a new suit later is not natural. If partner's suit
is a major, it will be a cue bid agreeing
partner's suit.*

SLAM BIDDING

4NT inquiry "Blackwood"

After partner's diamond opening and jump raise in spades, it is fair to assume that you do not have a third-round club loser. Whether you can make 11, 12, or 13 tricks just depends upon how many aces partner holds. You can find out by bidding 4NT, Blackwood.

YOU	PARTNER
	1 ♦
1 ♠	3 ♠
4 NT	

You will therefore sign off in 5♠ if partner bids 5♦ (one ace), bid 6♠ over 5♥ (two aces), and bid 7♠ over 5♠ (three aces).

THE RESPONSES TO 4NT	
5 ♣	ZERO OR FOUR ACES
5 ♦	ANY ONE ACE
5 ♥	ANY TWO ACES
5 ♠	ANY THREE ACES

When partner asks for aces, you have no choice about how to continue. You must show the number you hold; here, one. Voids do not count as aces, though an experienced partnership would have an agreement about how to show a void.

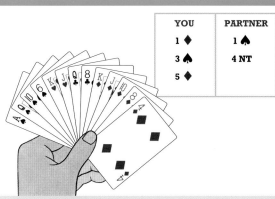

YOU	PARTNER
1 ♦	1 ♠
3 ♠	4 NT
5 ♦	

IMPORTANT POINT *Avoid using Blackwood if you have two fast losers in a suit or a void somewhere. Unless your side has all four aces, the reply will often leave you guessing.*

Continuations after 4NT

After you have used Blackwood and found out that your side has all the aces, you may continue with 5NT to ask for kings. If partner has a king, you can be sure of 12 tricks, and there are so many chances for a 13th that you will bid the grand slam. Partner may have a doubleton club or a useful queen. Even if not, you might set up a long spade.

YOU	PARTNER
	1♠
3♥	4♥
4 NT	5♥
5 NT	

THE RESPONSES TO BLACKWOOD 5NT	
6♣	ZERO OR FOUR KINGS
6♦	ANY ONE KING
6♥	ANY TWO KINGS
6♠	ANY THREE KINGS

When partner follows 4NT asking for aces with 5NT asking for kings, you normally show the number of kings according to the table shown. Here, with none, you bid 6♣. The one time you do not show your kings is if the knowledge that your side has all four aces enables you to count 13 tricks. Then you can just bid the grand slam.

YOU	PARTNER
1♠	3♥
4♥	4 NT
5♥	5 NT
6♣	

IMPORTANT POINT *Many duplicate players prefer Roman Keycard Blackwood. In this variant, the trump king counts as an ace and the trump queen may also be shown.*

5NT inquiry

A bid of 5NT when not preceded by 4NT asks about partner's trump holding, specifically the ace, king, and queen. Usually known as the Grand Slam Force, it is perfect for a hand like this. If partner has the ace and king of trumps, you want to be in 7♦. If not, you will have to settle for the small slam.

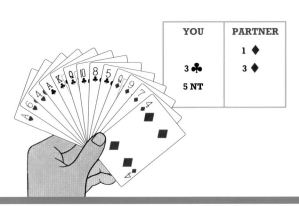

YOU	PARTNER
	1 ♦
3 ♣	3 ♦
5 NT	

There is not quite the same universal agreement about responses to the 5NT trump inquiry as there is to Blackwood.

RESPONSES TO TRUMP INQUIRY	
6 ♣	**NONE OF THE TOP THREE TRUMPS**
6 AGREED SUIT	**ONE OF THE TOP THREE TRUMPS**
7 AGREED SUIT	**ANY TWO OF THE TOP THREE TRUMPS**

The 5NT inquiry can follow an exchange of cue bids. It can also be used if one player has all the controls. When partner bids 5NT, you have little choice as to how to respond. With one top honor, you bid six of the inferentially agreed trump suit. The one exception is if you have so many trumps that your side has a known 12-card fit. Then, with the ace, you can jump to the grand slam.

YOU	PARTNER
1 ♦	3 ♣
3 ♦	5 NT
6 ♦	

IMPORTANT POINT *Some tournament players use 5NT for a very different meaning, asking partner to "pick-a-slam."*

The choice is usually between suits bid by the partnership.

Cue bids

With Blackwood, you show how many aces (and sometimes kings) you hold but not where they are. Cue bids are a way to show specific controls: aces, kings, voids, and singletons.

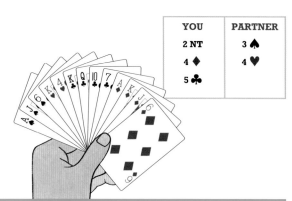

YOU	PARTNER
2 NT	3 ♠
4 ♦	4 ♥
5 ♣	

For a bid to be a cue bid, there are three conditions.
The other crucial difference between Blackwood and cue bids is that players exchange information rather than one of them asking questions and the other giving answers.

THREE CONDITIONS FOR A CUE BID

1. **YOU HAVE AGREED ANOTHER SUIT AS TRUMPS, EXPLICITLY OR, AS ABOVE, IMPLICITLY**

2. **YOU CANNOT STOP SHORT OF GAME**

3. **IF THE AGREED SUIT IS A MINOR, YOU HAVE GONE PAST 3NT**

On this auction, your 4♦ must be a cue bid agreeing spades because you would bid 3NT if you did not like spades. Since your 2NT indicated a balanced hand, it must mean the ace rather than a void. 5♣ is also a cue bid and, since you would have bid 4♣ rather than 4♦ if you held both minor-suit aces, it shows the ♣K. 4♥ by partner was another cue bid, but you cannot be sure whether it shows the ♥A or a void.

THE TRADITIONAL RULES FOR MAKING A CUE BID

1. **SHOW FIRST-ROUND CONTROLS (ACE OR VOID) FIRST**

2. **SHOW THE CHEAPEST CONTROL FIRST**

3. **ONLY MAKE A CUE BID IF A SLAM IS STILL A POSSIBILITY**

IMPORTANT POINT *Many tournament players make cue bids on first- and second-round controls in either order at the three* *or four level. They use 4NT later to check on aces.*

Raising to five of a major

Raising four of a major to the five level, or jumping to five of a major, is another way to look for a slam. In many auctions, where your side has bid three suits or if the opponents have bid a suit, it asks whether partner has first- or second-round control of the problematic suit. On this hand, your chances of making 6♠ are good unless partner also has two fast club losers.

YOU	PARTNER
1 ♦	1 ♥
1 ♠	4 ♠
5 ♠	

CONTINUATIONS AFTER A RAISE TO FIVE OF A MAJOR

5NT	**KING OF THE KEY SUIT**
CUE BID	**ACE OR VOID IN THE KEY SUIT**
6 AGREED SUIT	**SINGLETON IN THE KEY SUIT**
PASS	**AT BEST, THIRD-ROUND CONTROL OF THE KEY SUIT**

A jump to or advance to five of a major carries a different meaning if your side has bid only one or two suits naturally. In this instance, rather than focus on a particular side suit, it asks for good trumps. "Good" is a relative term. Partner's opening at the four level already suggests a fair seven- or eight-card suit, so you are looking for a potentially solid suit.

YOU	PARTNER
	4 ♥
5 ♥	

IMPORTANT POINT *Too many players take control in slam auctions with a 4NT inquiry. Often it works better to try for a slam in a* *way that involves partner in the decisions, such as cue bidding.*

Which slam try to make

If partner has around 20 points, your side could be in the slam zone. Although it is unlikely that there is a weak suit to worry about for a no-trump contract, it is better to show your club support than make an invitational raise to 4NT. In a club contract, partner may be able to ruff a heart in your hand or set up the spades by ruffing.

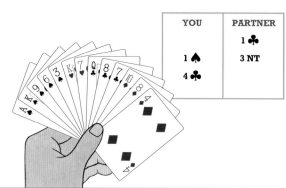

YOU	PARTNER
	1 ♣
1 ♠	3 NT
4 ♣	

It is rare that you can make a slam after a one-level opening and single raise (especially if you play strong twos). When a slam is makeable, opener is two-suited and responder needs some fit in the second suit. So jump in that suit, allowing partner to evaluate her diamond holding and give full weight to, say, the ♦K.

YOU	PARTNER
1 ♠	2 ♠
4 ♦	

Here, it would do you no good to cue bid one minor because partner will think you are looking for a control in the other. Nor will it help to ask for aces. What you really need from him is a good trump suit and a suitable hand for a slam. Your raise should convey this.

YOU	PARTNER
	1 ♥
1 ♠	3 ♥
5 ♥	

IMPORTANT POINT *Slam auctions can be hard to judge. A way to improve is to take 16 small cards out of a pack and practice bidding hands dealt from the remainder with your regular partner.*

OTHER SYSTEMS
Strong club systems

Rather than 2♣, some play that an opening of 1♣ is strong and artificial. This means that other openings are weaker. Two of the more common versions are Precision and Blue Club.

PRECISION	
The main features of traditional Precision are as follows:	
1♣	16+ HCP WITH 1♦ NEGATIVE OR NATURAL POSITIVE RESPONSES
1♦	11-15 HCP WITH NO FIVE-CARD MAJOR, A "CATCH-ALL" BID
1♥/1♠	11-15 HCP, FIVE-CARD MAJORS WITH FORCING 1NT RESPONSE
1NT	13-15 HCP
2♣	11-15 HCP, SIX CLUBS OR FIVE CLUBS PLUS A FOUR-CARD MAJOR
2♦	11-15 HCP, THREE SUITER SHORT IN DIAMONDS
2♥/2♠	6-10 HCP, SIX-CARD SUIT, "WEAK TWO"

BLUE CLUB	
The main features of traditional Blue Club are as follows:	
1♣	17+ HCP WITH 1♦ NEGATIVE OR CONTROL-SHOWING RESPONSES
1♦	12-16 HCP, MAY BE CANAPÉ (LONGER SUIT ELSEWHERE)
1♥/1♠	12-16 HCP, FOUR-CARD MAJORS AND MAY BE CANAPÉ
1NT	13-17 HCP, WITH LONG CLUBS IF 13-15
2♣	12-16 HCP, SIX CLUBS AND GENERALLY NO FOUR-CARD MAJOR
2♦	17-24 HCP, THREE SUITER WITH ANY SHORT SUIT
2♥/2♠	6-10 HCP, SIX-CARD SUIT, "WEAK TWO"

You make a game-forcing response of 1♠ in both systems. In Precision, it shows the five-card spade suit and, in Blue Club, it shows three controls (an ace counts as two and a king as one). If you were playing transfer responses (commoner now), you would bid 1♥.

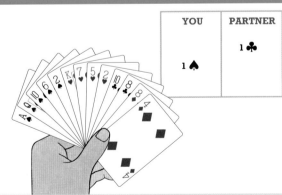

YOU	PARTNER
	1♣
1♠	

IMPORTANT POINT *If your opponents use a strong club system, discuss with your partner how to defend against it. If you allow the opponents a free run after 1♣, they will probably reach their best contract.*

Two-over-one game force

**A variation of standard bidding is
to play that a two-over-one
response** creates a game force.
When you have the values to do
this, it allows maximum room
for finding the best contract.
4♠ could be best if partner has a
singleton in hearts or clubs, but, in
standard methods, you would have
to rebid 3NT or risk missing game
if you rebid a non-forcing 2NT.

YOU	PARTNER
	1 ♠
2 ♦	2 ♠
2 NT	

**This time you can be almost
certain that you belong in hearts.**
Still, if partner has extra values,
you may have a slam, which a
jump to 4♥ could make difficult
to bid. After your single raise,
partner can cue bid (in case you
have extras) or perhaps bid 3NT
as a "serious" slam try.

YOU	PARTNER
	1 ♠
2 ♦	2 ♥
3 ♥	

**The downside to having two-level
responses** as game forcing is that
you must respond 1NT on a
wide variety of hands. 1NT,
in response to a major, is thus
forcing. Opener must find a rebid,
bidding a three-card minor if need
be. As responder, you will bid
again with 10–12 points.

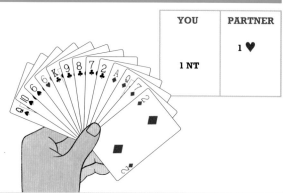

YOU	PARTNER
	1 ♥
1 NT	

IMPORTANT POINT *If you play two-over-
one, it is important that you and your partner
agree what subsequent actions show extra*
*values. Otherwise, you will get out of your
depth or miss slams.*

Benjamin

Playing weak twos and strong twos are mutually exclusive—or are they? A Benjamin 2♣ opening shows 21–22 balanced or a strong two in any suit. You will show your long suit, if any, on the next round.

YOU	PARTNER
2♣	2♦
3♦	

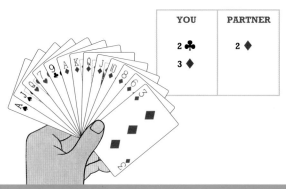

Since a 2♣ opening in Benjamin shows a hand slightly weaker than it does in standard methods, you need a different bid for the strongest hands. This is 2♦. The negative response is 2♥. The Benjamin 2♦ is forcing to game unless opener rebids 2NT over 2♥.

YOU	PARTNER
2♦	2♥
2♠	

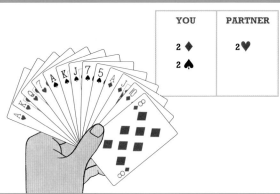

Since you can rebid 2NT having opened 2♣ or 2♦ with 21–22 and 23–24 respectively, a 2NT opening is available to show 19–20.

YOU	PARTNER
2 NT	

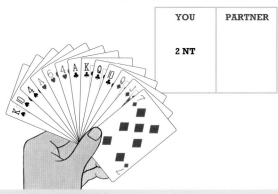

IMPORTANT POINT *The loss of a natural 2♦ opening is minimal. The bigger snag is that the 2♣ opening is vulnerable to opposing preemption.*

Multi

The Multi is a different way to allow you to show both weak and strong two hands. 2♦ shows either a weak two in a major or various strong hands. By agreement, the strong hands are either three suited (when you rebid in the suit below the singleton) or, as shown here, a strong two in a minor.

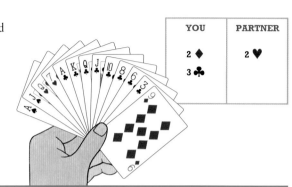

YOU	PARTNER
2 ♦	2 ♥
3 ♣	

Unless she has a weak hand with a long string of diamonds, responder may not pass 2♦. Usually she makes a relay bid of 2♥. You then pass with a weak two in hearts, bid 2♠ with a weak two in spades, or bid higher with a strong hand.

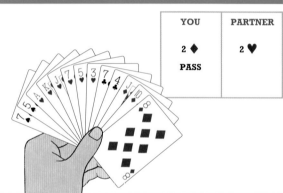

YOU	PARTNER
2 ♦	2 ♥
PASS	

If partner opens a Multi and you have enough to foresee game facing a weak hand, you can inquire with 2NT. Partner's rebid will typically show whether he is maximum or minimum and whether he has hearts or spades. Like Benjamin and strong club systems, the Multi is only played in duplicate.

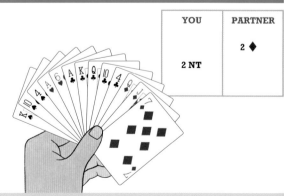

YOU	PARTNER
	2 ♦
2 NT	

IMPORTANT POINT *The Multi has many advantages. The main snag is that the other side has two chances to bid: directly over 2♦ or on the second round.*

OVERCALLS
Basic requirements

At the one level, you can overcall on a weaker hand than you need for an opening bid. Vulnerable, you need perhaps 11 points and non-vulnerable you can reduce that slightly. On a marginal hand, look at your long suit. With a good suit, the chance of being doubled is less, and it is more likely to be a good lead for partner.

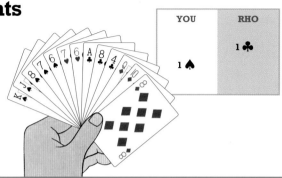

YOU	RHO
	1♣
1♠	

At the one level, a five-card suit is fine for an overcall. Since there is a much higher chance of being doubled at the two level, you look for a six-card suit if possible and at least 11–13 points. Remember as well that there is less room to find alternative contracts.

YOU	RHO
	1♥
2♣	

With a suit as poor as these diamonds it would be highly unwise to overcall at the two level. Indeed, you would probably pass even if RHO had opened 1♣, which would give you the chance to bid at the one level. Apart from the risk of being doubled, it is unlikely that you want to sacrifice in diamonds or have the suit led.

YOU	RHO
	1♥
PASS	

IMPORTANT POINT *An overcall is a good way to help find the best contract if the deal belongs to your side or to direct the lead and make life difficult for the other side if it does not.*

Raising an overcall

Whether or not you play five-card major openings, an overcall indicates a five-card suit, so you can freely raise with three trumps. This increases the chance that your side will buy the contract as well as making life even more difficult for the other side. The range for a single raise is about 6–10 points.

YOU	LHO	PARTNER
	1♣	1♠
2♠		

With four trumps and around 11–12 points, you are entitled to give a jump raise. Please note, however, that many duplicate players treat a jump raise as weak (though still showing four-card support). They tend to have special conventions to show a hand like this.

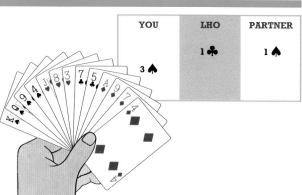

YOU	LHO	PARTNER
	1♣	1♠
3♠		

With five trumps and 13 points (3 for the singleton) you can raise partner's overcall straight to game. If it does not make, the opponents can surely make something. Again, duplicate players tend to play a raise to game as shapely but weak (the same hand without the ♦A) and might make a splinter bid of 4♣ on this hand.

YOU	LHO	PARTNER
	1♣	1♠
4♠		

IMPORTANT POINT *Raising partner is even more important on a competitive deal because it helps your side stay in the auction while continuing to cut out bidding space for the opponents.*

Advancing without a fit

The upper limit for an overcall is about 17 points, which means you do not need to strain to keep the bidding open as much as when facing an opening bid. Facing a one-level overcall, the range for 1NT is about 9–11 HCP and for 2NT is about 12–13 HCP. You will usually want at most two cards in partner's suit and a stopper in opener's suit.

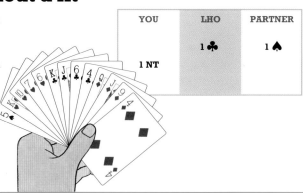

YOU	LHO	PARTNER
	1 ♣	1 ♠
1 NT		

In the old days, a change of suit after partner's overcall was a weak move. Now it is common to play it as constructive. You need at least 8 points to bid a new suit at the one level, and at least 11 to bid it at the two level. In addition, unless your suit is a major and partner's is a minor, you want to have a better suit than partner might have.

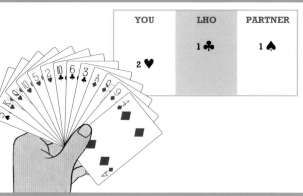

YOU	LHO	PARTNER
	1 ♣	1 ♠
2 ♥		

Since the lower limit for partner's two-level overcall is about the same as for an opening bid, you can safely bid 2NT with 11–12 points or 3NT with 13–15. Needless to say, you need to have a stopper or two in the opponent's suit.

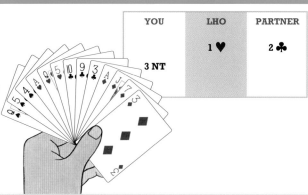

YOU	LHO	PARTNER
	1 ♥	2 ♣
3 NT		

IMPORTANT POINT *Since a one-level overcall may be weaker than an opening bid, you need to exercise caution in continuing the auction without a fit.*

Suit bids after their overcall

When an opposing overcall prevents you from responding at the one level, you need more values to respond than usual. Opener, if he wishes to repeat his own suit, will have to do so at the three level. Therefore, in this situation, you need at least 11 points to bid a new suit.

YOU	PARTNER	RHO
	1 ♣	1 ♠
2 ♥		

When you can make the response that you would have made without the overcall, you generally do so. Unless you have already passed or have a specific agreement with your partner, any change of suit response is still forcing after the overcall.

YOU	PARTNER	RHO
	1 ♣	1 ♥
1 ♠		

One bid that a simple overcall will never stop you from making is a single raise of partner's suit. This makes it an even more common action than usual. On this hand, you would have bid 2♥ playing five-card majors even without the overcall.

YOU	PARTNER	RHO
	1 ♥	2 ♣
2 ♥		

IMPORTANT POINT *If your response is above two of opener's suit, you need good values, enough to invite game. With less, you may have to pass or raise with less than normal support.*

Other bids after their overcall

When an opponent overcalls, partner will have another chance to bid, which means you need not strain to keep the bidding open. The lower limit for a 1NT response thus becomes a good 7 points, with a stopper in the suit overcalled.

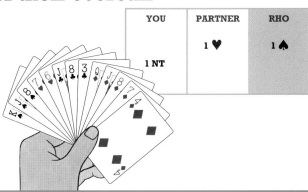

YOU	PARTNER	RHO
	1 ♥	1 ♠
1 NT		

With a strong responding hand and no suit you can show—2♥ would show five hearts—you can bid the opposing suit. This type of cue bid does not promise any particular holding in the suit bid. Unless you play negative doubles (see below), what else could you do with this hand?

YOU	PARTNER	RHO
	1 ♦	1 ♠
2 ♠		

Most duplicate players play negative doubles. This double shows not a desire to defend but four cards in the unbid major, hearts. Without this convention, you would bid 2♣, which is far from ideal, especially since partner may have three clubs and four hearts.

YOU	PARTNER	RHO
	1 ♣	1 ♠
DOUBLE		

IMPORTANT POINT *Many duplicate players use a cue bid of the suit overcalled to promise support for the suit opened rather than as a general force.*

1NT overcall

A 1NT overcall is very much like a strong 1NT opening. The range is 15–17 or, particularly over a major, 15–18 HCP. You need to have at least one stopper in the suit opened. Partner bids as if you had opened a strong 1NT.

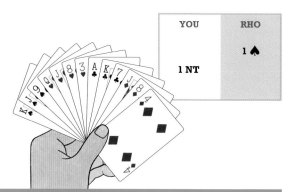

YOU	RHO
	1 ♠
1 NT	

You rarely overcall 1NT when holding a doubleton in the suit opened. When you do, you need a strong doubleton. A 1NT overcall is much better than introducing the mediocre clubs.

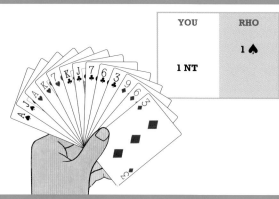

YOU	RHO
	1 ♠
1 NT	

Placing partner with a minimum of 15 points, you happily raise to game. You do not, of course, go looking for a four–four fit via Stayman in the suit that an opponent has opened.

YOU	LHO	PARTNER
	1 ♥	1 NT
3 NT		

IMPORTANT POINT *There is not the same taboo about overcalling 1NT with a singleton as there is in opening 1NT with one. It may be a lesser evil than overcalling with a weak suit or passing.*

Handling their 1NT overcall

An opponent who overcalls 1NT will tend to have tenaces over the opening bidder and a useful holding in opener's suit. This suggests caution for responder. Without the overcall you would have raised to 2♠, and you can still raise even with it.

YOU	PARTNER	RHO
	1♠	1 NT
2♠		

You would have bid 1NT yourself if RHO had passed, but now there is no need to keep the bidding open. Partner will have another chance to bid. Without support for partner, a long suit of your own, or sufficient values to double, you can only pass.

YOU	PARTNER	RHO
	1♠	1 NT
PASS		

With at least 9 HCP you usually double 1NT. This means that with a good suit you can bid two of a new suit on a weak hand. The bid is not forcing. Indeed, since your hand tends to be similar to that for a weak two, more often than not partner will pass.

YOU	PARTNER	RHO
	1♥	1 NT
2♠		

IMPORTANT POINT *A 1NT overcall radically changes your responses. You double with a strong hand if you do not mind defending, while a bid of 2NT suggests a shapely two-suited hand.*

Strong jump overcalls

Traditionally, a single jump overcall has shown a strong hand. You need at least a six-card suit and a hand better than a minimum opening bid. Typical ranges are 15–17 HCP and a six-card suit or 13–15 HCP with a seven-card suit. Since the bid is natural and limited, it is not forcing.

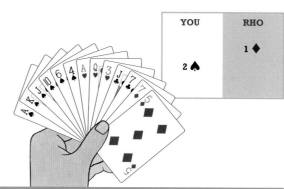

YOU	RHO
	1 ♦
2 ♠	

A strong jump overcall can be at the two level or the three level. In terms of playing strength, you will tend to have six to seven tricks at the two level and seven tricks at the three level. Since you are unlikely to be doubled, the vulnerability has little impact on the range.

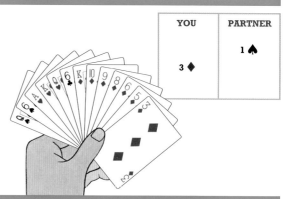

YOU	PARTNER
	1 ♠
3 ♦	

If partner makes a jump overcall, it is unlikely that you have a better suit than he does. You will therefore tend either to raise his suit if it is a major or look for 3NT if it is a minor.

YOU	LHO	PARTNER
	1 ♠	3 ♦
3 NT		

IMPORTANT POINT *Some duplicate players use intermediate jump overcalls, which are about 2 points weaker than the strong variety. This intermediate range comes up more often.*

Weak jump overcalls

Many duplicate players have abandoned strong jump overcalls altogether. A weak jump overcall at the two level is very much like a weak two opening. You have a six-card suit and about 5–9 HCP.

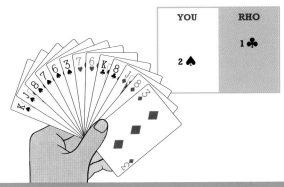

YOU	RHO
	1♣
2♠	

A weak jump overcall at the three level is similar to a weak three opening. Especially when you are vulnerable, you will want to have a seven-card suit for the bid. At both the two level and three level, you are trying to disrupt the opponents' bidding while describing your hand so that partner can judge if a sacrifice will be worthwhile.

YOU	RHO
	1♥
3♣	

If partner had dealt and opened 3♣, you would have passed. Therefore, you do the same facing a weak jump overcall. To try 3♠ (forcing) or bid 3♥ (asking for a heart stopper) would be highly optimistic.

YOU	LHO	PARTNER
	1♥	1♣
PASS		

IMPORTANT POINT *If you play weak two openings, you may like weak jump overcalls as well. They enable you to disrupt the opposing auction but can be revealing if you end up defending.*

Multiple jumps

Although a single jump overcall can be strong, intermediate, or weak by agreement, a jump of two or more levels is always preemptive in nature. You would have opened this hand 4♠ and so make the same bid as an overcall.

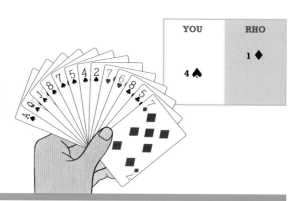

YOU	RHO
	1♦
4♠	

With extreme shape like this, you want to take up as much bidding space as possible. Even if you had a weak jump overcall of 3♦ available, the double jump is fine. Indeed, if only the other side is vulnerable, you might bid 5♦ on this hand.

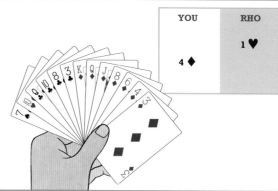

YOU	RHO
	1♥
4♦	

With this hand, you expect to make nine tricks. Therefore, even if you are vulnerable, you are within two tricks of your bid. Remember, in a sound style, you want to be within two tricks if you are vulnerable and within three tricks if you are not vulnerable.

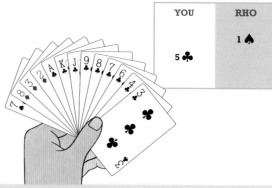

YOU	RHO
	1♠
5♣	

IMPORTANT POINT *Multiple jump overcalls are very much like preemptive openings. You take a calculated risk of conceding a penalty in order to make life tough for the opponents.*

Cue bids

Traditionally (and it is still the case in social games), a bid of the enemy suit, a cue bid, shows a very strong hand. It is equivalent to an opening of 2♣. Partner has to keep the bidding open until you reach game.

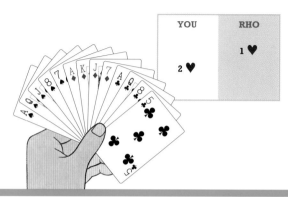

YOU	RHO
	1♥
2♥	

A jump cue bid has a special meaning. It shows a source of tricks (the running diamond suit) and asks partner to bid 3NT with a stopper in opener's suit or otherwise allow you room to show your suit.

YOU	RHO
	1♥
3♥	

Duplicate players use a cue bid for a different meaning, to show a hand with at least five cards in two unbid suits. If opener opens a minor, the two suits are the majors, and if opener opens a major, they are the other major and an unspecified minor.

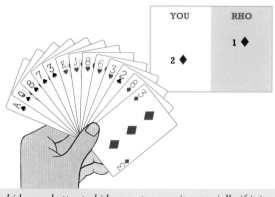

YOU	RHO
	1♦
2♦	

IMPORTANT POINT *If you use the cue bid to show a two-suited hand, you want to hold values in your long suits. If not, it may be better to bid your strong suit, especially if it is a major, or to pass.*

Unusual 2NT

Since you rarely have 20 points when an opponent opens, a 2NT overcall in second seat is not natural. It shows at least five cards in each of the two lowest unbid suits. These will be the minors if they open a major, or hearts and the other minor if they open a minor.

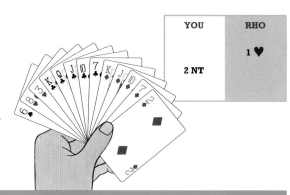

YOU	RHO
	1 ♥
2 NT	

The strength for an unusual 2NT is normally as on the first hand, looking to compete the part-score and make life hard for the other side. You can also have a hand like this, on which you plan to bid again if partner gives simple preference to one of your suits.

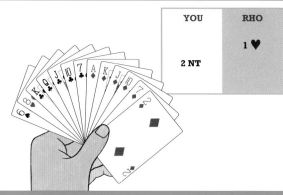

YOU	RHO
	1 ♥
2 NT	

By showing two suits at once, you double the chance of finding a fit. In addition, by showing hearts as well as diamonds, there is a better chance of getting to game. Even when 1♣ may be a three-card suit, 2NT still shows the two lowest unbid suits.

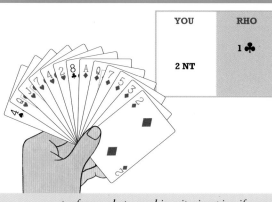

YOU	RHO
	1 ♣
2 NT	

IMPORTANT POINT *If partner bids an unusual 2NT, you invariably express preference between his suits, jumping if you have positive support.*

Sandwich seat

When both opponents are bidding
and they are bidding different
suits, you must be careful. More
often than not, your side will
be outgunned and the deal
may be a misfit. Unless your
suit is very good, you need
as much to overcall after an
opposing opening bid and
change of suit response as
you would to open.

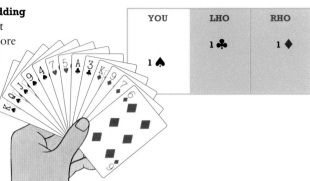

YOU	LHO	RHO
1 ♠	1 ♣	1 ♦

The range for a 1NT overcall in
the sandwich seat (so called
because you are sandwiched
between two opponents)
increases to 16–18.
In addition, as here,
it is desirable to have
stoppers in both bid
suits and a source of
tricks of your own.

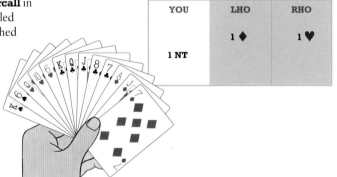

YOU	LHO	RHO
1 NT	1 ♦	1 ♥

**Sometimes the opposing opening
and response** mean that you
cannot show your suit at the two
level. You might have been
happy to overcall 2♣, but
3♣ is too risky on this
type of hand. You
would want a seven-
card or robust six-card
suit to bid.

YOU	LHO	RHO
	1 ♥	2 ♦
PASS		

IMPORTANT POINT *Most tournament
players play that an overcall in responder's
suit is natural and not a cue bid. You*
*invariably need a six-card suit to be sure that
you have greater length than responder.*

Protective (balancing) position

When an opponent passes a one-level opening, your partner should have some values. Even if the deal does not belong to your side, you want to push the opponents up a level or two. The rule is to mentally add a king to your hand and consider whether you would have bid in second seat. This gives you an easy 1♠ overcall.

YOU	LHO	RHO
	1♦	PASS
1♠		

The three points rule in the protective/reopening/balancing seat applies equally to a 1NT overcall or takeout double. The range for 1NT comes down to 12–14—some play it even weaker than this!

YOU	LHO	RHO
	1♥	PASS
1 NT		

Whether you play weak or strong jump overcalls in second seat, it is clear that there is no need to preempt opponents who are trying to stop at the one level. In fourth seat, jump overcalls are intermediate: a six-card suit and 13–15 points or a bit less with a seven-card suit.

YOU	LHO	RHO
	1♥	PASS
2♠		

IMPORTANT POINT *Beware of bidding strongly, especially on a misfit, if partner bids after two passes. He may already be bidding some of your values.*

Reopening after their overcall

If you open, LHO overcalls, and two passes follow, you will usually bid again unless yours was a minimum opening or you have length in the suit overcalled. The strength on the deal is probably divided evenly and you do not want to sell out too cheaply. On this hand, your six-card heart suit is clearly rebiddable.

YOU	LHO	RHO
1 ♥	1 ♠	PASS
2 ♥		

When you are short in the overcaller's suit, you will often reopen with a double because this is the most flexible action. Here, when you do not want to hear a spade bid from partner, 2♦ is better.

YOU	LHO	RHO
1 ♥	2 ♣	PASS
2 ♦		

With a balanced hand, you need considerable strength to bid again after an overcall. Playing a strong 1NT opening, a rebid of 1NT shows 18–19 points—possibly 17 in a hand unsuitable for a 1NT opening.

YOU	LHO	RHO
1 ♣	1 ♥	PASS
1NT		

IMPORTANT POINT *If you play negative doubles, you reopen more freely than if you do not. Responder, with length in the overcaller's suit, may have passed on as many as 11 or 12 points.*

Bidding after their preempt

Preempts from the opponents are designed to make life difficult. To avoid being shut out of the auction, the accepted rule is to put your partner with a balanced 8 points and bid accordingly. Here, with your decent six-card major, the prospect of making game if partner can raise just justifies the overcall.

YOU	RHO
	3 ♦
3 ♠	

Since on the previous hand you might make a simple overcall, you need to act more strongly when you have eight tricks or so, as here. This action might be to double before showing your suit or, as on this hand when you have a seven-card suit but only 14 HCP, by jumping in your suit.

YOU	RHO
	3 ♦
4 ♠	

Since it means taking 11 tricks, making game in a minor is often difficult. It is no easier after an opposing preempt. If you have a stopper in the preemptor's suit and an overcall in your long suit would be at the four level, it is generally better to try 3NT.

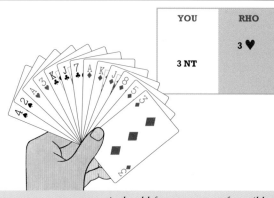

YOU	RHO
	3 ♥
3 NT	

IMPORTANT POINT *An opposing preempt does not improve your hand. On the contrary, it should forewarn you of possible bad breaks.*

Advancing after their preempt

If partner overcalls (or doubles) an opposing preempt, he is probably bidding about the first 8 of your points. Therefore, to bid higher you need more. This hand is an ace or king more than the assumed 8, and you like spades, so you raise to game.

YOU	LHO	PARTNER
	3 ♦	3 ♠
4 ♠		

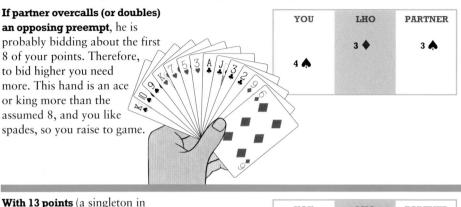

With 13 points (a singleton in partner's suit is no asset), you have more than enough to bid on. Since you do not like spades but do have a diamond stopper, you bid 3NT.

YOU	LHO	PARTNER
	3 ♦	3 ♠
3 NT		

Aces are always an asset, and the fact that you can show your long suit without increasing the level makes it worth showing. You hope that partner can raise hearts or, with a club stopper, bid 3NT. Your change of suit bid is forcing.

YOU	LHO	PARTNER
	3 ♣	3 ♦
3 ♥		

IMPORTANT POINT *If partner comes in after an opposing preempt, he is generally playing you for some values. To bid on to game you need about 10 points or more.*

TAKEOUT DOUBLES
When a double is for takeout

In each of these auctions (the list is not exhaustive), the double requests a takeout. The doubler should have support or, in the last case, tolerance for any unbid suits, or be strong enough to rectify matters if his partner bids a suit that he does not like. A takeout double is often the best way to enter (or stay in) the bidding.

YOU	LHO	PARTNER	RHO
	1 ♦	DOUBLE	

YOU	LHO	PARTNER	RHO
			1 ♦
PASS	1 ♥	DOUBLE	

YOU	LHO	PARTNER	RHO
	1 ♠	PASS	2 ♠
DOUBLE			

YOU	LHO	PARTNER	RHO
	1 ♠	PASS	PASS
DOUBLE			

YOU	LHO	PARTNER	RHO
1 ♠	2 ♦	PASS	PASS
DOUBLE			

IMPORTANT POINT *A double by you is for takeout, asking partner to bid, if one, your partner has taken no positive action in the bidding and two, the double is of a suit contract below game or of a 1NT in response to an opening bid.*

Initial doubles

A takeout double of a one-level opening suggests 12 HCP upward with a singleton in the suit opened, 10+ HCP with a void in the suit, or 13+ HCP with a doubleton in the suit. The more minimum you are, the more important it is that you have support for all unbid suits. With this hand, you are happy whatever suit partner bids.

YOU	RHO
	1♠
DOUBLE	

A 5–4–3–1 type, short in the suit opened, is normally suitable for a takeout double unless you have five cards in one major and less than four in the other. Swap the hearts and clubs on this hand and you would overcall 1♠.

YOU	RHO
	1♦
DOUBLE	

When the opponents bid two suits, you need at least eight cards and preferably nine in the other two suits to make a takeout double. You also need sound opening bid values because you cannot be sure of finding a fit.

YOU	LHO	PARTNER	RHO
	1♦	PASS	1♠
DOUBLE			

IMPORTANT POINT *Gone are the days when you might double on any opening hand. Unless you have 18 points or more, a takeout double should deliver a fair dummy in any unbid suit.*

Showing a suit after partner's double

Partner, in doubling for takeout, is asking you to bid. Other things being equal, you show a longer rather than a shorter suit and a major rather than a minor. With a weak hand (0–5 points) and both majors, you bid hearts. With some values, you can bid again if the opponents compete, so here you show spades first.

YOU	LHO	PARTNER
	1♣	DOUBLE
1♠		

Since partner's double forces you to bid, you need to have a way of showing genuine values. A jump response shows about 9–10 points and invites partner to raise with anything extra.

YOU	LHO	PARTNER
	1♣	DOUBLE
2♠		

Although your best suit is spades, you stand little chance of beating 1♠ doubled. Therefore you bid your longest other suit, in this case diamonds.

YOU	LHO	PARTNER
	1♠	DOUBLE
2♦		

IMPORTANT POINT *After partner's double, a minimum response suggests 0–8 points, a single jump 9–10 points, and a double jump in a major 11–12. Avoid big jumps on four-card suits.*

Advancer's cue bid and double

Here you easily have the values to jump to 2♠, but doing so could miss a heart fit. To show two or more places to play and at least the values to invite game, you bid the opposition's suit. This action is forcing until your side agrees (bids and raises) a suit.

YOU	LHO	PARTNER	RHO
	1♣	DOUBLE	PASS
2♣			

Often, responder will bid after partner's double, in which case you can pass. If you wish to compete and show that you can play in more than one denomination, make a "responsive double" over RHO's raise. A responsive double does not promise as much strength as a cue bid and you can pass partner's next bid. Here, though, you would correct 2♠ to 3♣.

YOU	LHO	PARTNER	RHO
	1♥	DOUBLE	2♥
DOUBLE			

IMPORTANT POINT *With a game-going hand after partner doubles, start with a cue bid (or responsive double if responder raises opener) unless you are sure that you know the best place in which to play.*

No-trump bids and penalty pass

If your only biddable suit is opener's or you have only a weak minor, it might be right to bid 1NT. You normally need a good holding in the suit opened and about 7–10 points. With fewer values, it is best to bid a suit, even if it is only a three-card suit. Turn the ♥A into a small heart and you would bid 2♣.

YOU	LHO	PARTNER
	1 ♠	DOUBLE
1 NT		

A jump to 2NT after partner's double shows about 10–12 points. It is likely to be the best move if you have length in the suit opened or a strong three-card holding and a balanced hand with no major.

YOU	LHO	PARTNER
	1 ♣	DOUBLE
2 NT		

There is one time that you do not remove a take-out double. This is when you have real length and strength in the suit opened. Even if the opponents are playing five-card majors, you are likely to have better hearts than opener and so are happy to choose the suit as trumps.

YOU	LHO	PARTNER
	1 ♥	DOUBLE
PASS		

IMPORTANT POINT *Someone who makes a takeout double frequently has a singleton in the suit opened. Keep this in mind before leaving the double in or making a no-trump bid.*

Rebids having doubled

With a minimum double, you will always have tolerance for partner's suit and can pass. Bidding 1NT or a new suit on the next round shows real extra values. Since you would have bid 1NT on the first round with 15–17 HCP, 1NT following a double shows a stronger hand, with 18–19 or 18–20, like the one shown.

YOU	PARTNER	RHO
		1 ♦
DOUBLE	1 ♥	PASS
1 NT		

After your double, when partner bids a suit you really like, you might want to raise. Since she may have had to bid on a Yarborough, you bid with more restraint than if you had opened. A single raise shows about 16–18 points, a double raise 19–20, and a jump to game 21–22.

YOU	PARTNER	RHO
		1 ♦
DOUBLE	1 ♠	PASS
3 ♠		

Since partner will often bid a four-card suit after your double, you do not raise with only three-card support. If, as here, you cannot bid 2NT (or 1NT) for lack of a stopper in opener's suit or bid a suit of your own, the only choice left is a cue bid. This shows 18 points upward.

YOU	PARTNER	RHO
		1 ♠
DOUBLE	2 ♥	PASS
2 ♠		

IMPORTANT POINT *You might raise when not quite so strong either to avoid being shut out of the auction (if opener bids again) or if partner has promised some values by bidding freely.*

Raising after their double

When one opponent makes a takeout double, the other is going to bid and they are likely to find a fit. You want to make this as hard as possible for them. The rule is that, if you have four-card support, you bid one level higher than you would without the double. This means a double raise shows 6–10 points and a single raise may have less.

YOU	PARTNER	RHO
	1 ♠	DOUBLE
3 ♠		

The rule that you do not make a jump raise with only three-card support still applies. It is not safe to go leaping around when you have only a moderate fit, especially when there is a higher chance than usual of a bad break, as indicated by the takeout double.

YOU	PARTNER	RHO
	1 ♠	DOUBLE
2 ♠		

Since a jump raise after the double shows a maximum of 10 points, you need another way to show game invitational values or better. 2NT is a conventional bid to show a good raise to three or better. You do not need 2NT as a natural bid because you would redouble with a strong balanced hand.

YOU	PARTNER	RHO
	1 ♥	DOUBLE
2 NT		

IMPORTANT POINT As opener, if partner raises you after an opposing double, bear in mind that she is likely to be weaker than *if she had made the same bid without the double.*

Other ways of handling their double

With a good hand (one too strong for a 1NT response) and no particular fit for partner, you redouble. Often you will be happy to double an opposing contract, so opener only bids at his next turn with a shapely minimum.

YOU	LHO	RHO
	1 ♠	DOUBLE
REDOUBLE		

On the basis that you can redouble with a good hand, many people play that a change of suit is not forcing after a double. This hand is tailor-made for that. However, many duplicate players do play that a new suit is forcing, in which case they would pass this hand planning to bid diamonds at their next turn.

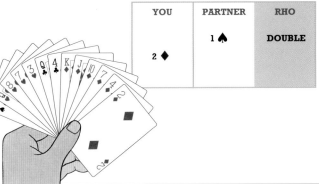

YOU	PARTNER	RHO
	1 ♠	DOUBLE
2 ♦		

After a double, the lower end of the range for a 1NT response increases slightly, say to 7 points. In addition, since the doubler will often have four cards in any unbid major, you can bid 1NT if it feels right rather than showing a moderate four-card major at the one level.

YOU	PARTNER	RHO
	1 ♥	DOUBLE
1 NT		

IMPORTANT POINT *If you play a change of suit as forcing after a double, a redouble indicates a definite interest in defending. If not, this inference is less clear.*

Continuing with a double

If you start with an overcall and wish to bid on the next round even though partner has not bid, it is often

YOU	LHO	PARTNER	RHO
			1 ♦
1 ♠	2 ♦	PASS	PASS
DOUBLE			

right to double. This suggests tolerance for any unbid suits, certainly if there were any higher in rank than your own. It would be highly unusual for you to bid your suit a second time with fewer than six cards in it.

If responder raises opener's suit, a second double is also for takeout. The lowest bid that partner can

YOU	LHO	PARTNER	RHO
			1 ♥
DOUBLE	3 ♥	PASS	PASS
DOUBLE			

make after your double is 3♠, so you need a hand good enough to have jump raised if LHO had passed. This means about 19 points or more.

On the first round, your hand was ill-suited for a double because of the singleton heart. Now that

YOU	LHO	PARTNER	RHO
			1 ♣
PASS	1 ♥	PASS	2 ♥
DOUBLE			

the opponents have found a fit in hearts, you can double on the second round.

IMPORTANT POINT *A takeout double is often the most flexible action, keeping the bidding low and giving partner the option to defend.*

Protective doubles

If an opponent opens and his partner passes, you can apply the same rule as you do with a protective

YOU	LHO	PARTNER	RHO
	1 ♠	PASS	PASS
DOUBLE			

overcall—mentally add a king to your hand. 13 HCP and a singleton would be more than enough to double in second seat, so this hand is fine for a balancing double.

If you open, LHO overcalls, and two passes follow, you will often want to compete when short in the suit

YOU	LHO	PARTNER	RHO
1 ♥	2 ♣	PASS	PASS
DOUBLE			

overcalled. A takeout double gives partner the chance to bid a new suit, put you back to your suit, or defend. If you play negative doubles, partner may well want to play for penalties and exercise the last option.

A double is much better than bidding one of the major suits. If partner bids 2♦, you will correct

YOU	LHO	PARTNER	RHO
1 ♥	2 ♣	PASS	PASS
DOUBLE			

to hearts. If not, you normally will have lost nothing.

IMPORTANT POINT *Doubles in the protective/reopening/balancing seat have become very popular with duplicate players. Having the right shape is key.*

PENALTY DOUBLES
When a double is for penalties

On each of these auctions (the list is not exhaustive), the final double is for penalty, expressing the view that the opponents will not make their contract. In the last auction, partner's first double is for takeout and you made a penalty pass. This counts as a "positive action," making partner's second double for penalties.

YOU	LHO	PARTNER	RHO
1 ♥	2 ♣	DOUBLE	

YOU	LHO	PARTNER	RHO
1 ♣	PASS	1 ♠	2 ♦
DOUBLE			

YOU	LHO	PARTNER	RHO
	1 NT	DOUBLE	

YOU	LHO	PARTNER	RHO
	1 ♠	PASS	1 NT
PASS	2 ♠	DOUBLE	

YOU	LHO	PARTNER	RHO
	1 ♦	DOUBLE	PASS
PASS	2 ♣	DOUBLE	

IMPORTANT POINT *A double is for penalties if the doubler's partner has taken positive action, if it is of a no-trump bid (other than a 1NT response), or if the doubler's earlier inaction precludes a takeout interpretation.*

Safety margin

The hand below satisfies all three conditions and, if you play penalty doubles in this position, double is fine.

YOU	PARTNER	RHO
	1 ♠	2 ♥
DOUBLE		

THREE CONDITIONS FOR A SUCCESSFUL PENALTY DOUBLE AT A LOW LEVEL

1. **LENGTH AND STRENGTH IN THE OPPOSING TRUMP SUIT**

2. **FEW CARDS IN PARTNER'S LONG SUIT**

3. **SUFFICIENT VALUES FOR YOUR SIDE TO HAVE THE BALANCE OF POWER**

At the three level, a strong four-card holding in the opposing trumps suit normally suffices for condition 1. A doubleton in a suit in which partner probably has only five cards is also fine for condition 2. When you have an opening bid and partner has the values to respond at the two level, it is clear that this hand meets condition 3 as well.

YOU	LHO	PARTNER	RHO
1 ♠	PASS	2 ♥	3 ♦
DOUBLE			

IMPORTANT POINT *Only double the opponents when you expect to defeat their contract by two tricks. This gives you a safety margin of a trick if they turn up with unexpected shape.*

Standing partner's double

Some players would retreat to 2♠ on the basis that they have six spades and only one heart. This is poor

YOU	LHO	PARTNER	RHO
1♠	2♥	DOUBLE	PASS
PASS			

thinking. If LHO has enough hearts to overcall in the suit and partner enough to double at the two level, you normally will have only one heart. Instead, count the assets of two aces and your ability to stand a spade lead.

Partner's low-level penalty double does not demand that you pass. This hand has two serious defensive

YOU	LHO	PARTNER	RHO
1♠	2♥	DOUBLE	PASS
2♠			

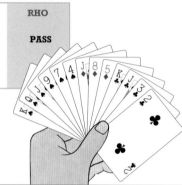

flaws. For one, you have no aces. For another, you have no hearts. A void in trumps is bad because dummy may have a few and you can never lead them.

Many players go astray here, thinking that 1NT doubled will make. It may, but you will often be in

YOU	LHO	PARTNER	RHO
	1 NT	DOUBLE	PASS
PASS			

more trouble if you bid. With a balanced hand, it is invariably right to pass partner's penalty double of 1NT.

IMPORTANT POINT *If partner's penalty doubles follow normal rules of prudence, you only need to take them out when your hand is unexpectedly weak defensively.*

Standing an opponent's double

Although you do not much care for partner's diamonds, it would be a mistake to run to 3♣. For one thing, you may well be swapping one 6–1 fit for another while raising the level. Also, LHO may be about to remove the double.

YOU	LHO	PARTNER	RHO
	1♠	2♦	DOUBLE
PASS			

The situation alters when partner opens 1NT and the opponents double for penalties. Partner should have tolerance for any suit you bid. This hand may be worthless in 1NT but produce three tricks with clubs as trumps. Most people play that 2♣ is natural after a double, not Stayman, meaning that you can retreat into clubs. It is also common, if you play them, that transfers no longer apply.

YOU	LHO	PARTNER	RHO
		1 NT	DOUBLE
2 ♣			

IMPORTANT POINT *Many players run too quickly from the frying pan into the fire when an opponent doubles. If your side is in trouble, you generally want to keep the bidding as low as possible.*

Lead-directing doubles

At the slam level, there is little mileage in doubling just for the sake of turning 50 into 100 or 100 into 200 when there is so much more to lose if the slam makes. The rule is that if you are not on lead then a double by you asks for an unusual lead. Here you want a diamond lead so that you can score a ruff to go with your ♣A. The double conveys this message because, with hearts and clubs unbid, a lead of one of those suits would not be unusual.

YOU	LHO	PARTNER	RHO
			1 ♦
PASS	2 ♠	PASS	3 ♠
PASS	4 NT	PASS	5 ♠
PASS	6 ♠	PASS	PASS
DOUBLE			

Assuming the opponents can count up to 25, it is very unlikely that you would want to double on the basis of overall strength, and all the more so when you could not bid over 1♠. The double here again asks for an unusual lead, usually dummy's first bid suit—although it is true that a lead of declarer's suit would be more unusual still!

YOU	LHO	PARTNER	RHO
	1 ♦	PASS	1 ♠
PASS	1 NT	PASS	3 NT
DOUBLE			

IMPORTANT POINT *The odds are very different when contemplating a lead-directing double. It is worth taking a chance to defeat a contract that you expect would make on the wrong lead.*

Penalty redoubles

Bridge differs from poker and backgammon in that it is rare for the stakes to keep going up. If the opponents only double when they expect to beat you by two tricks, it will be very rare for you to feel confident that the contract will make. When you are, you must be aware of the possibility that, if you redouble, they may escape to a cheaper spot, taking a sacrifice. Here you can deal with a retreat to 4♥; even facing a weak jump overcall, you expect to make 3NT. Of course, you do not want partner to bid 4♣, which might happen if you fail to redouble.

YOU	LHO	PARTNER	RHO
	1 ♥	3 ♣	PASS
3 NT	PASS	PASS	DOUBLE
REDOUBLE			

Whatever the strength of 1NT, the same principles apply. By redoubling (a) you tell partner that your side has the balance of power and that he can double if LHO retreats, and (b) this converts a part-score contract into a game.

YOU	LHO	PARTNER	RHO
		1 NT	DOUBLE
REDOUBLE			

IMPORTANT POINT *An opponent who doubles often has a surprise in store. Beware of redoubling unless you are confident of making your contract and can cope if opponents run to a sacrifice.*

SOS redoubles

Because of the likelihood that an opponent will retreat if you make a penalty redouble, it is normal to play that redoubles of very low-level contracts (other than 1NT) are for rescue. Here, if partner has three cards in one of the red suits, you expect playing in that suit to be better than 2♣ doubled. There is also the possibility that they cannot double your side in two of a red suit.

YOU	LHO	PARTNER	RHO
	1 ♠	2 ♣	DOUBLE
REDOUBLE			

Whether or not 1♣ could be a short suit, it would be silly for you to redouble because you liked clubs. You would be content to play in the contract doubled rather than defend. With this three-suited hand, you are happy for partner to bid any of the other three suits. It would also work to redouble if you just had length in the majors. If partner bids diamonds and they double, you could redouble again!

YOU	LHO	PARTNER	RHO
		1 ♣	PASS
PASS	DOUBLE	PASS	PASS
REDOUBLE			

IMPORTANT POINT *SOS redoubles only apply at a low level and when your side has not found a fit. Beware of redoubling* *for rescue if you think partner might misunderstand your intentions!*

COMPETITIVE DECISIONS
The law of total tricks

In the diagram below both sides have a nine-card fit, North–South in spades and East–West in hearts. This implies a total of 18 tricks. This is right: North–South make nine tricks with spades as trumps and East–West nine tricks with hearts as trumps. The rule still works if you trade the ♣A and ♣10 or the ♦A and ♦10. In the first case, East–West make ten tricks while North–South can make only eight. In the second, North–South take ten tricks to their opponents' eight.

If, instead, you trade the ♥3 and the ♠3, both sides will have a ten-card fit. Then you will find that both sides can make ten tricks.

> **THE LAW OF TOTAL TRICKS**
>
> 1. **COUNT THE NUMBER OF TRUMPS ONE SIDE HAS IF IT PLAYS THE CONTRACT**
> 2. **DO THE SAME FOR THE OTHER SIDE AND ADD THEM TOGETHER**
> 3. **THE TOTAL SHOULD BE THE SAME AS THE NUMBER OF TRICKS EACH SIDE CAN TAKE IN THEIR RESPECTIVE CONTRACTS**

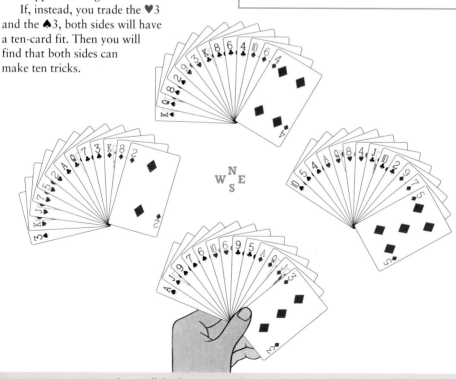

IMPORTANT POINT *Almost all duplicate players use the law of total tricks to a certain extent. Although it can be a trick* *off one way or the other, it is much better than relying on guesswork.*

Decisions at particular levels

You have six spades and know that partner has at least three. If the values are equally split between the two sides, this suggests you can make nine tricks with your nine-card fit. Selling out to 3♥ is only likely to be right if the cards lie badly for your side and your bid pushes the opponents into a makeable game.

YOU	LHO	PARTNER	RHO
			1 ♥
1 ♠	2 ♥	2 ♠	3 ♥
3 ♠			

You have three spades and partner surely one or none. This gives the opponents a nine- or ten-card fit. Partner has shown 5–5 at least in the minors and, if he is 6–5, he is more likely to have six clubs than six diamonds. In the worst but likeliest case, their side has a nine-card fit and yours an eight-card fit. 17 trumps suggest 17 tricks. So, if 4♠ makes, a sacrifice in 5♦ doubled will be defeated by four tricks. This will be a losing action at any vulnerability.

YOU	LHO	PARTNER	RHO
	1 ♠	2 NT	4 ♠
PASS			

IMPORTANT POINT *When you are in genuine doubt about who can make what, it pays to bid one more. Trading +50/100 for -50/100 is small compared to losing a game when you could have made one.*

When to sacrifice

After partner's preempt, there is no doubt that 4♠ will make. It is also reasonable to hope that he has a singleton spade, in which case you will have just three aces to lose. Although it is true that 6♠ might make, the opponents are just as likely to bid it if you pass.

YOU	LHO	PARTNER	RHO
		3 ♦	4 ♠
5 ♦			

THREE CONDITIONS FOR A PROFITABLE SACRIFICE

1. **THE OPPONENTS WOULD MAKE THEIR CONTRACT**

2. **THE PENALTY IN YOUR CONTRACT WILL COST LESS THAN THIS**

3. **IT WILL NOT DRIVE THE OPPONENTS TO A HIGHER-SCORING, MAKING CONTRACT**

Partner's single raise could easily be with only three-card support, which means your side may have only nine trumps. The opposing fit, too, could be six–four but might easily be of only nine cards. This makes it highly likely that one or both of 4♥ and 4♠ will fail. All the same, you should bid 4♠ whatever the vulnerability. Unless LHO has the ♣K, you need very little from partner to give 4♠ good play. The chance it will make compensates for the times when it turns out to be a phantom sacrifice.

YOU	LHO	PARTNER	RHO
1♠	2♥	2♠	4♥
4♠			

IMPORTANT POINT *If you sacrifice and the opponents bid one more, it is usually right neither to double nor to bid again. If they go one down, you are doing well anyway.*

Doubling sacrifices

When your side has the balance of power and bids game, it is fair to assume that a higher bid by an opponent is a sacrifice. Therefore, you normally want to double to make the penalty as big as possible. You do not want to play in five of a major very often because there is no gain compared to being in four of a major and often a loss.

YOU	LHO	PARTNER	RHO
1 NT	PASS	4 ♠	5 ♣
DOUBLE			

Partner's strong jump shift makes it clear, even though you have not reached game, that RHO's bid is a sacrifice. Holding a singleton heart, you do not want to encourage partner to bid on. Of course, she may have diamond support, in which case she will remove your double. Partner will also remove the double if she has such a great hand that your side has a slam on. Compared to a double of an ordinary contract, a double of a sacrifice says, "I do not think we can make a higher contract," more than simply, "They cannot make theirs."

YOU	LHO	PARTNER	RHO
1 ♦	PASS	2 ♥	4 ♠
DOUBLE			

IMPORTANT POINT *Many players are overly reluctant to accept a penalty of lower value than the game or slam they could have made. "Take the money" is often good advice when they sacrifice.*

Bidding one more

Here, you have an exceptionally good hand for playing in spades. You have good trump support, fast winners in the red suits, and no wasted values in partner's likely short suit, clubs. Unless her 4♠ bid was extremely speculative, you can expect there to be good play for 5♠. Indeed, because your hand is such a suitable dummy, it might even be better to cue bid 5♦.

YOU	LHO	PARTNER	RHO
1 NT	PASS	4 ♠	5 ♣
5 ♠			

Partner's jump shift creates a game force, which means there is no question of letting the opponents play in 4♠ undoubled. A pass from you is therefore forcing. Since you would double if you wanted to defend, it invites partner to bid again. There is an inference that you have heart support because you could bid five of a minor if your interest in going on was based on strong diamonds or a minor two-suiter.

It is common to play that a two-over-one response creates a forcing pass situation as responder had promised to bid again anyway over opener's rebid.

YOU	LHO	PARTNER	RHO
1 ♦	PASS	2 ♥	4 ♠
PASS			

IMPORTANT POINT *If your side has announced game values, a pass over an opposing sacrifice is forcing. If you pass and then remove partner's double, this is a slam try.*

Chapter Three
The Play

OPENING LEADS

Top of a sequence

The opening lead is the most important card a defender plays. As the opening leader, your choice will often determine the contract's fate. One of the best leads is from a three-card honor sequence, such as K–Q–J–x–x, Q–J–10–x–x–x, or J–10–9–x. The lead is both safe (unlikely to concede a trick) and attacking (likely to set up winners for your side).

Another good lead, particularly against a suit contract, is from a suit in which you have the A–K. You can lay down a top card, knowing that, unless an opponent is void, it will win the trick. Having seen dummy and partner's signal, you can often work out the best defensive strategy. The old-fashioned method is to lead the king from A–K. The problem is that partner does not know whether to encourage with J–x–x (right if you have K–Q–x), or with a low doubleton (right if you have A–K–x and a ruff is possible). The other downside is that leading the king from A–K encourages people to lead suits in which they have the ace without the king—not normally a good idea.

IMPORTANT POINT
Some play that you lead the ace from A–K and others if you want partner to encourage if holding Q–x–x. They lead the king for a count signal if there is no chance that three rounds of the suit will stand up.

A three-card sequence with one card almost touching is also quite good. Lead the queen from Q–J–9–x, the jack from J–10–8–x, and the ten from 10–9–7–x–x. A two-card sequence is less attractive because it will often cost a trick if partner has no values in the suit. A lead from 10–9–x is safer than one from J–10–x or Q–J–x. A lead from K–Q–x is very risky. A lead from a suit in which you hold the K–Q is safer if you hold length in the suit and it also helps to hold the nine. Lead the card in bold:
K–Q–J–x–x, **K**–Q–10–x–x, **Q**–J–10–x, **Q**–J–9–x,
J–10–9–x–x–x, **J**–10–8–x–x–x, **10**–9–8–x, **10**–9–7–x,
A–K–Q–x, **A**–K–J–x, **Q**–J–x, **K**–Q–x

Exceptions to top of a sequence

Against a no-trump contract, you do not lead high from a two-card sequence if you have length in the suit (and you generally lead long suits against no-trump contracts). Suppose you lead ace, king, and a third heart. You have set up the suit, yes, but you will not score the long cards unless you have a side entry. Leading low from holdings like K–Q–x–x–x or Q–J–x–x–x will avoid blocking the suit. Also, doing so increases the chance that you will knock out a stopper while partner still has a card to let him return the suit. Note, however, that with precisely A–K–x–x it is usually right to lead high whatever the contract.

Layout
1

With A–K doubleton, you lead the king rather than the ace. This way, when you play the king followed by the ace, partner knows that you have no more cards in that suit. If, instead, you cashed the ace followed by the king and switched to another suit, partner might assume that you did so because you saw no future in the first suit.

Some people also play what are known as "alarm clock leads." A lead of the king from A–K says to partner "sit up and take notice." Often the message is that the opening leader is switching to a singleton or has a void somewhere. Indeed, if you have a void, you might underlead a sequence or start with your second-highest card to increase the chance that partner will win the first trick.

Layout
2

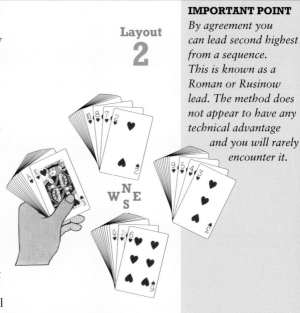

IMPORTANT POINT

By agreement you can lead second highest from a sequence. This is known as a Roman or Rusinow lead. The method does not appear to have any technical advantage and you will rarely encounter it.

Partner's suit

If partner has bid a suit, you usually lead it. By leading partner's suit, you will generally be leading toward strength (a good idea) and be either setting up or cashing tricks. Indeed, certain bids, such as some overcalls or light opening bids in third seat, are specifically designed to encourage the lead of the suit.

Layout **1**

Layout **2**

In a no-trump contract, you have added reason to lead partner's suit. Partner, evidently with strength to bid, is likely to have entries to cash any long cards that you might set up. The fact that an opponent presumably has a stopper should not deter you. The normal lead is low from three to an honor, here the two.

Another good reason to lead partner's suit is that a speculative lead in some other suit may catch partner with a worthless holding. You may then find that you have given away both a trick and a tempo. The lead of a club (clearly a suit partner has not bid if this is the layout) gives declarer a third club trick and achieves nothing.

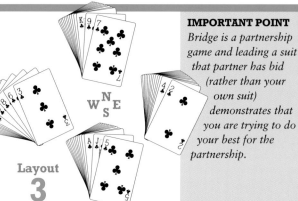

Layout **3**

IMPORTANT POINT
Bridge is a partnership game and leading a suit that partner has bid (rather than your own suit) demonstrates that you are trying to do your best for the partnership.

Not leading partner's suit

With a very poor hand, you can believe that the opponents have game values and that defending "normally" will

YOU	LHO	PARTNER	RHO
		1 ♠	2 ♥
PASS	4 ♥	END	

not be enough. On this sequence, you should lead your diamond. Partner may have the ace there and perhaps the ♠A as well and give you two ruffs. Your weakness increases the chance that partner has entries.

Again, you have good reason not to lead partner's suit. You have a good suit of your own and an entry to it.

YOU	LHO	PARTNER	RHO
		1 ♣	1 NT
END			

Moreover, someone who overcalls 1NT often has length and strength in the suit opened. When you are playing five-card majors, you have even more reason not to lead a club—partner may have only three clubs. Lead the ♠J.

When you have an attractive lead of your own, you can lead it in preference to partner's suit.

YOU	LHO	PARTNER	RHO
1 ♦	PASS	1 ♠	3 ♣
END			

This applies particularly when partner has not shown a strong suit. A response at the one level, a possibly prepared opening in one of the minors, or a simple response to your take-out double are all consistent with a weak suit for partner. Lead the ♦K.

IMPORTANT POINT *The more strongly partner has bid a suit, the more likely you are to lead it. When partner has only bid a suit once, and at a minimal level, that suit may be weak and you might lead your own suit instead.*

Interior sequence

A holding of two touching cards and a higher nontouching card is an interior (or broken) sequence. The card to lead is the highest of the touching cards—the ten from Q–10–9–x or K–10–9–x–x, the jack from K–J–10–x–x. With the layout shown, you can see that leading the ten enables the defenders to finesse against dummy's jack.

Layout **1**

Layout **2**

An interior sequence can have the ace at the top. In this case, you generally lead the suit only against a no-trump contract and with at least five cards in the suit. Lead the jack from A–J–10–x–x and the ten from A–10–9–x–x. On the layout shown, the jack knocks out South's stopper and lets the defenders run the suit if East gets in.

A lead from an interior sequence involves risk, often losing if partner has nothing. On a layout like this, it may also cost (dummy plays low), and the trick will not come back in a suit contract. For this reason, and because partner often cannot tell whether you have led your highest card, an interior sequence is often second choice.

Layout **3**

IMPORTANT POINT

Some play "strong ten" leads, in which case the ten shows an interior sequence (such as K–J–10–x–x or Q–10–9–x) and the lead of the jack or nine implies a weak holding. A further variant is "zero or two higher" leads, when any honor shows either zero or two higher honors.

Fourth highest

If you do not have a sequence and partner has not bid, it is often right to lead fourth highest of your longest and strongest suit. In a no-trump contract, you want to lead a long suit to set up long cards. In a suit contract, it is fairly safe to lead from length because declarer might ruff later rounds or discard losers on dummy's winners. Lead the ♠4.

Layout
1

Layout
2

Any small card would avoid blocking the suit. Why lead precisely fourth best? Partner can tell from the missing lower cards (if any) how long your suit is—with the three led and the two in dummy, he knows you have only four. If you had led the seven, partner might put you with one of the ♣3 or ♣5 and expect a five- or six-card suit more often than not.

Partner can also guess declarer's strength. The two closed hands must have nine higher cards if the card led is the two, eight if it is the three, and so on. (This is known as the "rule of 11.") The six lead leaves five higher cards, all of which East can see. Therefore, he can let the six run if dummy plays low (and is confident that the lead is not from Q–9–6).

Layout
3

IMPORTANT POINT
Some people lead fifth highest from a suit with an odd number of cards and third highest from an even number. Partner (and declarer) can then often tell at once if the lead is from a five-card suit.

Bad suits

With length (at least three cards) but no honor, it is advisable to lead your second-highest card. Why is this? If you lead high, you will have to follow downward and partner may place you with a doubleton and try to give you a ruff. If you lead low, partner may place you with an honor and go wrong, say by finessing against dummy.

Layout

1

W N E S

Layout

2

Partner can often work out a second-highest lead because the rule of 11 (see page 125) does not work. For the seven to be fourth best, you would need Q–10–9–7–(x) but, from that holding, you would lead the ten. Even the players (generally experts) who lead low from three cards lead second highest from longer bad suits.

If you have supported partner, the old-fashioned "top-of-nothing" lead has more merit. Partner already knows not to give you a ruff, so you can focus on showing whether you have strength in the suit. If you led the four, partner might finesse the jack (in case you have led from Q–9–4) at the cost of a tempo.

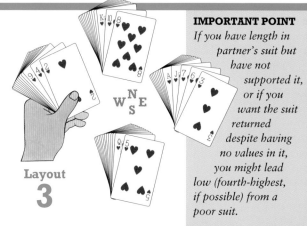

Layout

3

IMPORTANT POINT

If you have length in partner's suit but have not supported it, or if you want the suit returned despite having no values in it, you might lead low (fourth-highest, if possible) from a poor suit.

Short suits

A singleton lead can be good
against a suit contract. It
is best in a suit that the
opponents have not bid (or
you could be setting it up).
It is also best when you have
a weak hand and place
partner with an entry or two.
A further factor is your trump
holding. You do not want to
ruff with something like
Q–J–x, which would be a
trick anyway.

Layout **1**

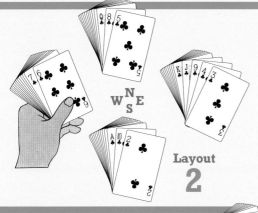

**You are less likely to score
a ruff by leading top of a
doubleton.** For one thing,
declarer (or dummy) may
have a doubleton as well and
have higher trumps than you
have. For another, partner
needs either two quick
winners in the suit or one
quick winner and a fast
trump entry. More often than
not, a doubleton lead is a
passive lead.

Layout **2**

**A lead from a doubleton
honor** is normally one to
avoid. Since you risk losing a
trick by leading into a tenace,
a split tenace, or a frozen suit,
you would often need a ruff
merely to break even. An
added danger is that, unless
partner can see the honor
immediately below the one
you lead, it will look as
though you have it.

Layout **3**

IMPORTANT POINT
*Most players go
looking for ruffs on
too many hands.
If you have an
attractive lead
elsewhere, it is
usually best to
prefer that.
Remember, a lead
from a short suit often
saves declarer a guess.*

Unsupported aces

The lead of or away from an unsupported ace (an ace without the king behind it) is generally a bad lead against a suit contract. You want to use your ace to capture a high card. You may lose the ability to do so if you attack the suit, as is the case in the diagram shown.

Layout **1**

If dummy has the king and declarer the jack in either hand, a lead away from an ace may put declarer to an early guess. Even so, there are many ways this can go wrong. There is no guess if partner has the Q–J, if declarer has the queen, or if an opponent has a singleton. It is rarely worth the risk of losing your ace.

Layout **2**

A lead from an ace risks confusing partner. Suppose you lead the two and dummy plays low. Partner, assuming you have led from the jack, will play the nine. As the cards lie, this will lose to the jack and give declarer one heart loser instead of two. Even if partner put up the king, declarer would make an undeserved third-round winner.

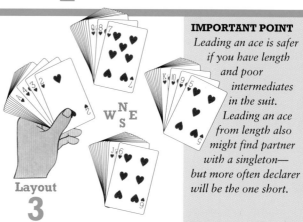

Layout **3**

IMPORTANT POINT
Leading an ace is safer if you have length and poor intermediates in the suit. Leading an ace from length also might find partner with a singleton— but more often declarer will be the one short.

Avoiding a trump lead

Trump leads have properly gone out of fashion. For one thing, if you blow a winner in a side suit, you may find that you would not have made it anyway because declarer could take a discard or a ruff. The same does not apply in the trump suit. A trump lead may go wrong on this hand if partner has any of Q–x–x, K–J–x, K–10–x, or A–J–x.

LHO	RHO
1 ♦	1 ♠
3 ♠	4 ♠

A trump lead is often too slow. On an auction like this, when you suspect that declarer can take discards on dummy's clubs, you need to set up or cash winners quickly. The best way to do this is to lead from your short strong diamond suit. While a trump is most unlikely to cost a trump trick, it may well cost your side's diamond tricks.

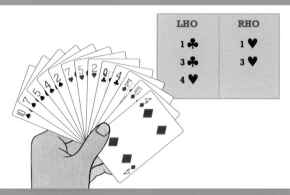

LHO	RHO
1 ♣	1 ♥
3 ♣	3 ♥
4 ♥	

A trump lead gives up the initiative. Remember that often the first thing declarer does is draw trumps. It follows that it cannot usually be right for the defenders to do so. By leading a side suit, you retain the option of setting up winners or cashing them or looking for a ruff. It is easy to imagine layouts on which any lead bar a trump would set the contract.

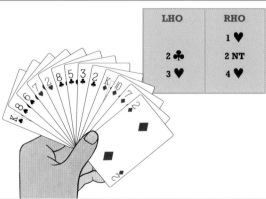

LHO	RHO
	1 ♥
2 ♣	2 NT
3 ♥	4 ♥

IMPORTANT POINT *Do not lead a trump when in doubt. Instead, look for a side suit in which a little help from partner will make it an effective lead.*

Winning trump leads

A strong holding in declarer's main side suit is a good reason to lead a trump. You can predict that dummy will be short in that suit and that declarer will try to ruff it. To cut down on dummy's ruffing value and so protect your spade holding you lead a trump. Note that it is normal to lead low from a doubleton in the trump suit.

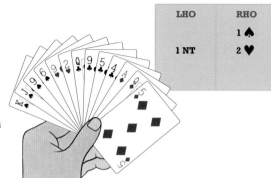

LHO	RHO
	1 ♠
1 NT	2 ♥

A series of tenaces in the side suits gives you another good reason to lead a trump. With most of the missing strength in declarer's hand, a lead away from any of your three kings is unattractive. Partner will need some strength somewhere for you to beat the contract, but you should not try to guess where it is. Lead a safe trump, the three for preference.

LHO	RHO
	2 NT
3 ♣	3 ♥
4 ♥	

If the opponents sacrifice with few high cards, they will be relying on ruffing winners to get close to

YOU	LHO	PARTNER	RHO
	PASS	1 ♥	1 ♠
2 ♣	4 ♠	DOUBLE	

their contract. In this hand, you have the minors and partner hearts, so how else can they make their tricks? Cut down on a potential crossruff with a trump lead, even though it is a singleton.

IMPORTANT POINT *A trump lead often proves effective in reducing the opponents' ruffing potential if they need many ruffs.*

Even if they need only one, perhaps your side has an entry in their short suits and can lead trumps again.

Unbid suits

The heart bid on your right should deter you from leading fourth-highest of your longest and strongest suit. Instead, you should lead your better of the unbid suits, spades. While partner could easily have length or strength in spades with you, a heart lead would surely only help declarer. Lead the ♠2.

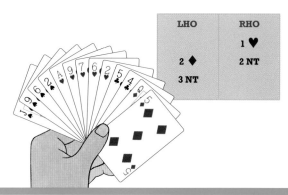

LHO	RHO
	1 ♥
2 ♦	2 NT
3 NT	

A lead from your A–K combination is not a good idea when dummy has shown five cards in the suit. The last thing you want to do is to help declarer to set up the hearts. Realistically your choice lies between the minors and, given your touching diamond honors, the ♦J is your best bet.

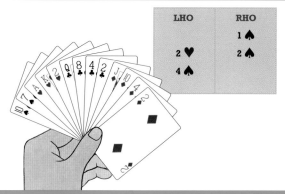

LHO	RHO
	1 ♠
2 ♥	2 ♠
4 ♠	

When there is only one unbid suit, you always consider leading it. On this auction, it seems like the opponents wanted to play in 3NT but could not do so for lack of a heart stopper. If this is the case, a heart lead may be both safe and necessary. Any other lead could enable declarer to discard a heart from one hand or the other. Try the ♥A.

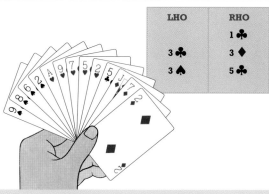

LHO	RHO
	1 ♣
3 ♣	3 ♦
3 ♠	5 ♣

IMPORTANT POINT *Opponents usually bid suits in which they have length and strength.* *A lead of such a suit will often either cost a trick or lose vital time.*

Choice of unbid suits

Other things being equal, you lead a major rather than a minor. This is because opponents will tend to bid their majors if they have them. On this auction, although RHO may have length in one of the majors, LHO would probably have used Stayman if holding a four-card major, so probably has length in the minors. This makes a spade lead best.

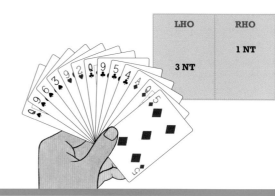

LHO	RHO
	1 NT
3 NT	

This time the clue lies in what your side has not done. Partner must have some values for you to be able to defeat

YOU	LHO	PARTNER	RHO
			1 ♣
PASS	1 ♥	PASS	1 NT
PASS	3 NT		

this contract, but was unable to overcall 1♠. If partner has a fair five-card suit, it is thus more likely to be in diamonds, a suit in which a one-level overcall was not possible, than in spades, in which it was.

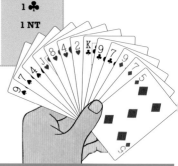

This looks like a three-way guess. You have three four-card suits, all with one honor and the nine. Experience has shown that a lead from a queen is better than one from a jack or a king. A lead from a jack often gets you nowhere and a lead from a king may cost a second-round winner. In the long run, a diamond from the queen should work best.

LHO	RHO
	1 ♠
1 NT	3 ♠
4 ♠	

IMPORTANT POINT *If the auction suggests a long suit in dummy, lead from a short strong unbid suit. If the auction suggests no rush to take quick winners, lead from a long or weak suit.*

Bid suits

Declarer, having bid two suits and shown a stopper in a third during this bidding, figures to be short in hearts. When you add this to the fact that you have an attractive sequence in hearts and a tenace in the unbid club suit, the heart lead stands out. It may not always work, but it is surely the percentage action to lead the ♥10.

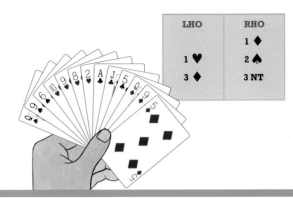

LHO	RHO
	1 ♦
1 ♥	2 ♠
3 ♦	3 NT

The bidding provides a big clue again. Given that the opponents have bid and raised diamonds, it is likely that they have eight cards in the suit. If this is the case, partner has a singleton and will be able to ruff the second round. You therefore lead the ♦A and plan to continue with the two as a suit-preference signal for clubs.

LHO	RHO
	1 ♥
2 ♦	3 ♦
4 ♥	

With a decent five-card suit and two possible entries, RHO's bid does not deter you from leading a spade, but it does affect which spade you lead. To avoid wasting a high card if dummy or partner has a singleton honor, or to avoid blocking the suit if partner has a doubleton honor, lead the four rather than the jack.

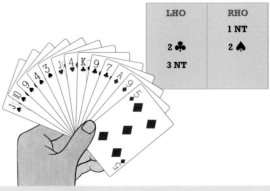

LHO	RHO
	1 NT
2 ♣	2 ♠
3 NT	

IMPORTANT POINT *Finding a killing lead may well depend on listening attentively to the bidding and applying the information learned in the context of your own hand.*

Small slam in suit

Opponents who bid a slam
should have an idea of how they
can get 12 tricks. Therefore, you
need to look for two tricks
quickly. Partner may have an ace
(or they might have bid seven)
and you want to set up a second
trick. A heart is best because your
suit is shorter than your clubs and
because you have the queen
rather than the jack.

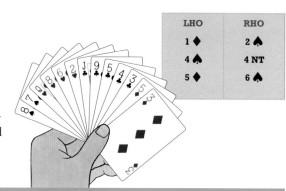

LHO	RHO
1 ♦	2 ♠
4 ♠	4 NT
5 ♦	6 ♠

**As a rule, you do not lead an
unsupported ace** against a slam
for the same reasons as in a lower
contract. Lead an ace only if you
think partner may have the king
or a singleton in the suit or when
(as here) you have a trump trick
or reason to place partner with
one. If you do not cash your ace
at trick one, it may be lost on
the clubs.

LHO	RHO
1 ♣	2 ♥
3 ♣	3 ♥
4 NT	5 ♥
6 ♥	

A club lead would be silly—if
partner can get in, the slam is
down anyway. A heart into
declarer's main suit is not much
better. Unless they have an
unlikely nine-card heart fit, this
will surely achieve nothing. The
best bet is the unbid diamond
suit. You can lead a second
round after getting in with your
trump ace and perhaps partner
can then ruff.

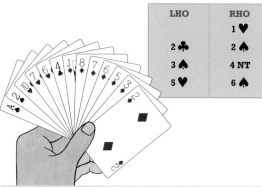

LHO	RHO
	1 ♥
2 ♣	2 ♠
3 ♠	4 NT
5 ♥	6 ♠

IMPORTANT POINT *If it sounds like the
opponents have balanced hands, you should
play passively, looking for a lead that should
give nothing away. Against most small slams
in a suit, however, the rule is to attack.*

No-trump slams

Opponents who bid to 6NT
usually have a lot of high cards
and all suits covered. The best
hope to beat them is usually to
hope that their hands fit poorly or
their finesses are wrong and give
nothing away. A lead from three
of the four suits in this hand
could easily cost a trick. A heart
lead is by far the safest. Most
would lead the nine rather than
the eight against 6NT.

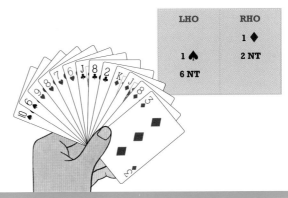

LHO	RHO
	1 ♦
1 ♠	2 NT
6 NT	

**A long worthless suit is often the
safest choice** even when an
opponent has bid the suit.
Remember, the more high cards
the other side has, the fewer
partner can have and the greater
the danger of leading from an
unsupported honor. Since dummy
can hardly be void in hearts, it
is very unlikely that a heart lead
will cost.

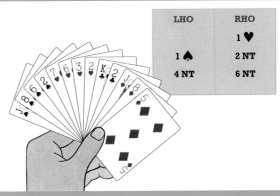

LHO	RHO
	1 ♥
1 ♠	2 NT
4 NT	6 NT

**The position changes when one
opponent** has a long suit. In this
case, you attack 6NT just as you
would a suit slam. If partner has
the club king and a quick entry
(maybe the ♦K), a club lead
will beat the contract. There is
little risk in this as the diamonds
are a source of tricks and any
finesses in the majors figure to
be working.

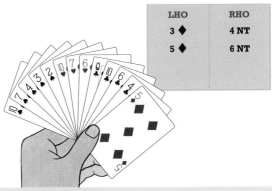

LHO	RHO
3 ♦	4 NT
5 ♦	6 NT

IMPORTANT POINT *Many players overbid
to 6NT when they have a lot of high cards
but no fit or shape. Do not let them get
away with it by gifting them a trick on the
opening lead.*

Grand slams

A trump is the traditional lead
against a grand slam. The thinking
is that the opponents rarely bid to
seven with a gap in their trump
suit. In addition, there is the
chance that you can save a ruff.
Here, all side suits look risky and
you should be happy to lead a
trump. You do not need to set up
winners because the contract is
down anyway if you get in.

LHO	RHO
1 ♦	2 ♠
3 ♠	4 NT
5 ♠	7 ♠

**Beware of leading a singleton
trump,** especially if the opponents
may be in a four–four fit (when
partner could hold J–x–x–x).
On this hand and this auction, a
spade lead is much safer than a
trump. Beware also of a trump
lead if partner could have Q–x–x.

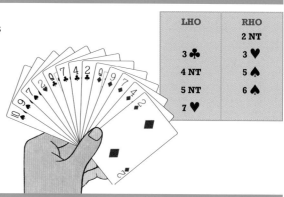

LHO	RHO
	2 NT
3 ♣	3 ♥
4 NT	5 ♠
5 NT	6 ♠
7 ♥	

Against 7NT, you normally look
for safety as well. You want to
avoid suits in which you or your
partner has an unsupported
honor. You rule out spades and
diamonds and, since LHO has
bid clubs, a club lead would be
much riskier than a heart. Even
if partner has J–x–x–x of hearts,
the opponents may have three
hearts each.

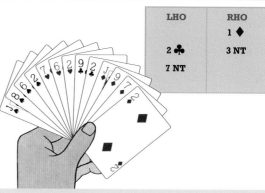

LHO	RHO
	1 ♦
2 ♣	3 NT
7 NT	

IMPORTANT POINT *If you have a safe
attacking lead, then make it—you might*
knock out a vital entry. If not, go passive
against a grand slam.

SUIT COMBINATIONS
Playing for the drop

Declarer can make four heart tricks if the queen is a doubleton. To take advantage of this situation you should cash the ace and king. It would not be good to lead the jack because West would cover and East's ten would win the third round.

Again, a finesse is not possible. You do not have the ♥J to go with the queen. You must therefore cash the ace in the hope that the king is a singleton. Leading the queen would be very poor, losing on the actual layout and creating an extra loser if East had the three missing hearts.

You could take a finesse here, after cashing the king, but it would not normally be a good idea. Playing the ace and queen next gains if East has either J–x or J–x–x. Finessing the ten is only essential to running five tricks if West has J–x–x–x, which is less likely. Finessing would be correct, however, with K–x facing only A–Q–10–x.

IMPORTANT POINT
Play to drop a missing high card with at least 11 cards (between the two hands) missing the king, nine cards missing the queen, or seven cards missing the jack.

Finessing

To score two tricks you finesse the queen (lead low and play the queen if the king does not appear), hoping that West has the king. If the lead is in dummy (North), you must first cross to the South hand in some other suit to do this. It is very often correct to lead toward the strong holding.

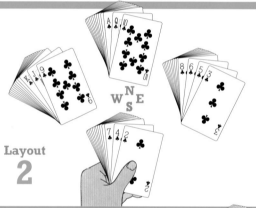

Layout **2**

To aim for three tricks you finesse the ten on the first round. You are finessing against two cards, the king and the jack. If the ten loses to the jack, you can finesse the queen next time and still make two tricks if West has the king. If West has the jack and East the king, the ten will drive out the king and you will have two tricks right away.

You can take a finesse even when missing the ace. You must lose to the ace of course, but you do not want to lose to the queen as well. Lead low to the ten. If this holds or loses to the ace, wait until you are back in your hand and then lead up to the jack.

Layout **3**

IMPORTANT POINT

A holding such as A–Q or A–K–J or K–J is known as a tenace. You want to lead toward this type of holding and hope that the missing high card(s) are under (in front of) the holding.

Avoiding a blockage

You have four certain heart tricks here. Cash the king, playing the seven from dummy, and the suit runs smoothly. It would usually be a mistake to cash the queen or (worse) the ace first. Then your king would win the second round and you would need a side entry to dummy in order to reach the remaining heart winners.

Missing the ace, again you lead high from the short hand. By leading the king, you can continue playing hearts until East takes the ace. If you led low to the queen (or led the queen), East could block the suit either by taking the ace on the first round or by ducking twice.

Layout
2

You can cope with a four–one break on this layout. You cash the king and lead to the ace, whereupon West shows out. This gives you a marked finesse against East's jack. You may be unable to run the suit, however, if you failed to unblock the ten under the king. East might duck the ten on the third round to leave you stranded in dummy.

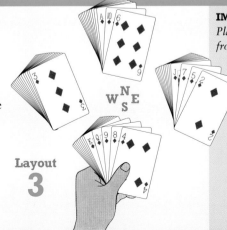

Layout
3

IMPORTANT POINT
Playing high cards from the hand with fewer cards in the suit first is the usual way to avoid a blockage in a suit.

Leading low

To make five tricks you need luck and skill. If you lead the jack, a competent West will cover with the king and East's ten will win the third round of the suit. The right play is to lead low and finesse the queen. On the next round, West's king falls to the ace to leave your jack a winner; dummy's remaining cards can score later.

Layout

1

You want West to play the ace on a low card. This way you can make three tricks even without a three–three break. Lead low from your hand and, assuming West plays low, put up the king. Then come back to your hand in some other suit and lead low again. West has to play the ace this time, so your king, queen, and jack all score.

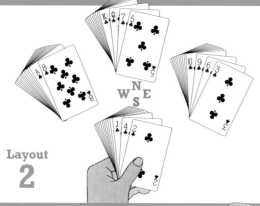

Layout

2

To have only one loser, lead a low heart from your hand. When West plays low, you finesse the ten. If this loses to the ace, you cash the king next. If the ten holds, come back to your hand and lead up to the king. With correct play, you will make three tricks if West holds either A–Q–(x) or, as shown, a doubleton queen.

Layout

3

IMPORTANT POINT
With many combinations, it is correct to lead a low card. This reduces the chance that you will have to play a high card from both hands on the same trick.

When to lead high

With ten cards missing the king, you intend to finesse.
It is best to lead the queen to do so because, when East covers and West shows a void, you will have a marked finesse against the ten. If you led low from dummy instead, East will not helpfully play the ten (or king). After finessing the jack, you would have a third-round loser.

Layout
1

If you need five tricks, you might succeed even if dummy has only the one entry. You start by leading the queen. If East covers, you capture the king with the ace and your remaining clubs are high. If, instead, the queen holds, the lead stays in dummy and you can take a second club finesse.

Layout
2

With only one entry to dummy again, you need to lead the nine. This will probably hold and you can lead the jack next. It would not work to lead the jack first. East could duck this and then you would have to win the second round in your hand. Nor would it help to lead the jack and drop the ten: East would then cover the nine.

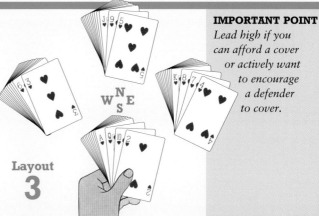

Layout
3

IMPORTANT POINT
Lead high if you can afford a cover or actively want to encourage a defender to cover.

Playing the right high card first

Declarer can make five heart tricks even if one defender holds all the missing hearts. You should cash the ace (or queen) first, leaving a tenace in both hands. Then you can finesse on the next round against whichever defender has four hearts.

South's hearts are weaker. This time, with the jack and ten missing, you cannot cater for four hearts with East. In case West has the length, start with the king. Then, with the position marked, you can lead twice toward dummy's A–Q–9 and just cover West's card each time.

Layout **2**

You are missing the queen, but to compensate you have ten cards between the two hands. You cannot do much about it if West holds Q–10–x, but you can deal with this holding in the East hand by laying down the ace.

Layout **3**

IMPORTANT POINT
The same idea applies if you are trying for one loser missing the ace. For example, holding K–Q–9–x–x facing J–8–x–x you lead the king, while with K–Q–8–x–x facing J–7–x–x you would begin with the jack.

Safety plays

If you need six tricks, then you finesse the queen, hoping that East has a doubleton king. If, however, five will suffice, you should cash the ace first in case West holds a bare (singleton) king.

Layout
1

If you need five tricks, then you lay down the ace in the hope that someone has a singleton king. Unfortunately, this play gives you two losers if West is void. The best play for at most one loser is to lead low from dummy, intending to finesse the ten if East plays the nine—you still avoid any loser if East has the singleton king.

Layout
2

If you can afford one loser, play the king first and lead toward dummy. You will play the nine if another low card appears, or play the ace if West shows out. This way you cope with any four–one split. To play for no loser you would cash the ace and finesse the jack. This gives you five tricks if East has the queen and the suit splits three–two.

Layout
3

IMPORTANT POINT

A related position is A–x–x opposite K–J–x–x. If you can afford one loser, play the king and ace, then lead to the jack. This works when Q–x–x–x–(x) is onside or the suit breaks three–three or the queen is doubleton.

Creating entries

North–South vulnerable
Dealer South

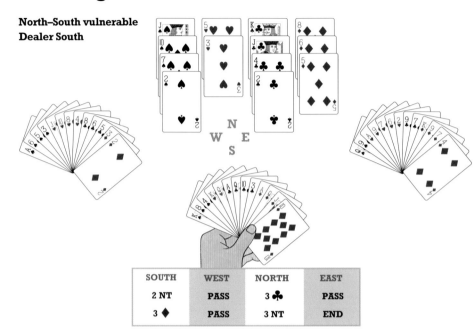

SOUTH	WEST	NORTH	EAST
2 NT	PASS	3 ♣	PASS
3 ♦	PASS	3 NT	END

West leads the ♥J, which East wins with the ace to return the six. What are your plans here?

What you know
If you lose the lead, you will go down, losing four hearts (at least) and the ♠A. Therefore, you must run nine tricks without losing the lead. These will have to be four diamonds, four clubs, and a heart. You hope that East has the ♦K, but entries could be a problem. If he has K–x–x–x, you will need to lead diamonds three times from dummy. The ♣K, ♣J, and ♣4 in dummy must all serve as entries.

The key plays
1. Having won the heart, cash the ♣A and lead the ♣10 to the jack, noting that all follow.
2. Lead a diamond to the queen, overtake the ♣Q with the king and repeat the diamond finesse.
3. Lead the ♣3 to dummy's four (!) and finesse again.

IMPORTANT POINT *If you had been short of entries to your hand, you could have led the ♣K to the ace, the jack to the queen, and the four to the ten. On a three–two break as above, the three could then be a fourth entry.*

Managing entries

Both sides vulnerable
Dealer South

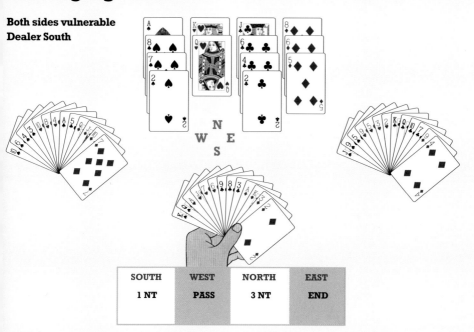

SOUTH	WEST	NORTH	EAST
1 NT	PASS	3 NT	END

West leads the ♦Q and, not being eager to have her switch to clubs, you win. What is your plan for nine tricks?

What you know

You have nine tricks on top—three spades, four hearts, and two diamonds. Both major suits are blocked, however, which means you need to be careful. The one entry you have outside of the blocked suits is to your hand in diamonds. This dictates that you play spades before hearts.

The key plays

1. You should cash the ♠K and ♠Q to unblock the spade suit.
2. Then cash the ♥K and ♥Q, which both unblocks the heart suit and puts the lead in dummy.
3. Next, cash the ♠A, discarding a losing diamond or club.
4. Finally, come to your hand with a diamond and cash the A–J of hearts.

IMPORTANT POINT *A suit like A–K–Q–3–2 facing 9–8–7–6 will be blocked on a normal three-one break. Discarding from the shorter holding can be the solution if there are no side entries to the long suit.*

Restricted choice

After you cash the king and the queen falls, you should finesse the ten on the next round. Although it is true that East could have been dealt a singleton queen or Q–J doubleton, with the latter holding he might equally have played the jack. The queen is more likely to be a forced play rather than one chosen from equals.

This time cashing the ace and king drops the ten. Again, it is more likely that East has had to play the ten from 10–x than that he has chosen to do so from J–10–x. Another way to look at it is to say in advance that you will finesse on the third round if the jack or the ten falls on the second. This loses only to J–10–x but not to J–x or 10–x.

Layout 2

On the first round you finesse the eight and the queen wins. Do you finesse the ten on the second round or do you put up the king? It is twice as likely that East was dealt either A–J–x or A–Q–x than Q–J–x, and the fact that you have seen the queen does not alter this. You should therefore finesse the ten.

Layout 3

IMPORTANT POINT
Whenever a defender plays a significant card, it is generally right to assume that he has done so out of obligation rather than choice.

Ducking

If dummy has no side entry
then you must duck one of the
first two rounds. On the
normal three–two break,
dummy's other four clubs will
all be winners. If three
winners would suffice (and
dummy is still entryless), it
could be right to duck twice
as a safety play against a
four–one break.

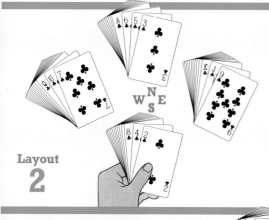

**You have less material to
work with here.** To set up one
long card you must hope for a
kindly three–three split.
Moreover, if dummy has no
side entry, you must duck
both the first and second
rounds of the suit. This leaves
the ace to serve as an entry to
the thirteenth club.

Even with no entry problems,
ducking can be a good idea. If
you play the ace, king, and
another heart to test for a
three–three break, someone
with four hearts (West) will
immediately be able to play
a fourth round. This may
mean that you cannot take
advantage of a helpful layout
in some other suit.

IMPORTANT POINT

*A–x–x–x–x opposite
x–x is another good
layout for
ducking. In a
suit contract,
you might later
cash the ace and
ruff the third round.
If the suit breaks three-
three, you have then set
up two long cards.*

Felling a high card

If you lead low to the king and it wins, you know who has the ace—West. It is therefore pointless leading up to the queen on the second round. Instead, you should duck completely. When West has a doubleton, this will force out the ace.

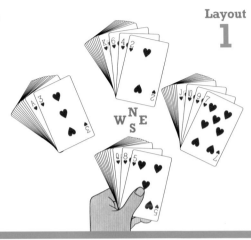

West's lead of the queen in a suit contract marks East with the ace. Rather than allow the ace to capture the king, play low from dummy. Later (or right away if West continues the suit), you can play a low heart from dummy and ruff out the ace. If East started with three hearts, you might still fell the ace but it would take two ruffs.

Layout
2

You lead the queen, which holds. If you need four tricks in the suit, there is no point in leading the six next. If East plays the king (having started with a doubleton), West will have the guarded ten. Instead, you should continue with the jack. East may fail to cover if West has three to the ten and there is nothing he can do when West has 10–x.

Layout
3

IMPORTANT POINT
Similar to the above holdings is K–x facing Q–x–x–x. If you lead to the king, intending to duck the second round and ruff the third, you make a second trick if there is A–x or A–x–x onside.

Probabilities

These probabilities (rounded to a whole percentage in some cases) apply if you know little about the unseen hands. You may notice that an odd number of cards tends to divide as exactly in half as possible, while an even number (other than two) does not.

You can work out the chance that a specific defender holds a certain number of cards by halving the relevant percentage. For example, if the East–West hands contain six hearts, the chance West has four hearts is half of the 48% for a four-two split, or 24%.

Remember that the chance a defender has any given card in a suit correlates to the number of cards held in the suit. If you are missing Q–x–x–x of hearts, and you know West has three hearts, West will hold the queen three-quarters of the time. This means that, if you do not know how the suit breaks, the probability West has Q–x–x is three-quarters of 25%, or 19%. In the same scenario, the chance East has Q–x is half of 40%, or 20%.

You can also combine chances by multiplying them together. If you need a two–two break and a winning finesse, your chance of success is 50% of 40%, or 20%. The table may also help you compare two lines of play. If one relies upon a three-two break and the other on a finesse (50% presumably), you do better to go for the former, a 68% chance.

DISTRIBUTION

TWO MISSING CARDS

1 – 1	52%
2 – 0	48%

THREE MISSING CARDS

2 – 1	78%
3 – 0	22%

FOUR MISSING CARDS

2 – 2	40%
3 – 1	50%
4 – 0	10%

FIVE MISSING CARDS

3 – 2	68%
4 – 1	28%
5 – 0	4%

SIX MISSING CARDS

3 – 3	36%
4 – 2	48%
5 – 1	14%
6 – 0	2%

CONTRACTS DEPENDING ON FINESSES

ONE FINESSE	50%
ONE OF TWO FINESSES	75%
TWO OF TWO FINESSES	25%
THREE OF THREE FINESSES	13%
TWO OF THREE FINESSES	37%

IMPORTANT POINT
You do not need to be a mathematician to play good bridge. The ability to count to 13 will see you through most situations.

GENERAL PLAY TECHNIQUES

Playing low in second seat

You should play low from dummy when West leads the four (unless you are desperate to have the lead in dummy). You would do the same if dummy had Q–x instead of J–x. East will have to play high to prevent your ten from scoring. After you capture the king with your ace, you will have another sure stopper.

With values in both hands, again it is right to play low from dummy when West leads a low heart. This way, your combined holding is bound to give you a stopper. You would have added reason to let the lead run around in a suit contract: West is much more likely to have led from the queen than the ace.

Layout
2

Even with quite a strong holding in dummy, it can still be right to let the lead come around to your hand. If you finessed the queen (the right play if you needed two fast diamond tricks), East will win with the king and you will make only one diamond trick. By playing low, East has to play the king on a low card and so you make the queen as well as the ace.

Layout
3

IMPORTANT POINT
Playing low in second seat can also be right even with A–Q–x in dummy facing small cards. If West has led a very low card, East will overtake and the A–Q will be protected.

When to play high in second seat

With a short suit in dummy and no intermediate cards or lesser honors in your hand, the rules change. Your only hope of making the queen is to play it at once on West's lead of the six. If East had the king, she would not play it on a low card but would instead try an intermediate card, such as the jack or nine.

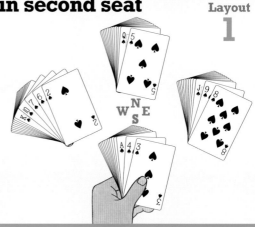

Here the holding in the closed hand is weak. If you play low from dummy and East is smart enough to play the ten (not so hard if he reads the lead of the two as showing an honor), you will not make a club trick. It is much better to put up the queen (or jack) to give you a trick if West holds either the ace or the king.

Layout 2

When West leads the nine, you can be sure East has the queen. It is therefore pointless playing low from dummy. By winning at once, you make it unsafe for East to return the suit and, in a suit contract, reduce the risk of a defensive ruff.

Layout 3

IMPORTANT POINT

In a suit contract, if you have a singleton in the suit led in your hand and dummy has the ace, it will very often be right to put up the ace.

Leading suits that set up winners

Both sides vulnerable
Dealer South

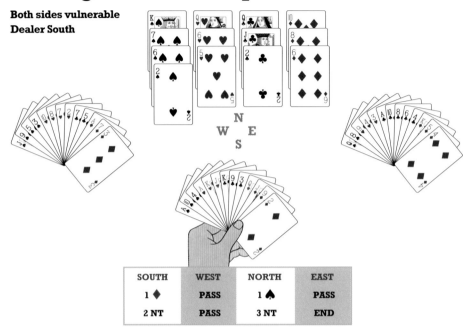

SOUTH	WEST	NORTH	EAST
1 ♦	PASS	1 ♠	PASS
2 NT	PASS	3 NT	END

West leads the ♥2 and your king wins. What is your plan to make this contract?

What you know

With only five top tricks (three hearts and two spades), you need four more. Both minors offer two sure winners once the missing high cards have gone, while spades offers the potential for only one extra trick, and that is not certain. To lead the ♥2 West must have only four hearts, so the suit is four–three and presents no real danger. A five–two club split, however, might pose a problem if you lead clubs too early.

The key plays

1. You should win the first trick in your hand and lead a diamond.
2. Win the next heart and persevere with diamonds.
3. Win the third round of hearts and drive out the ♣A. You now have nine tricks: two in each minor and the five top tricks you started with.

IMPORTANT POINT *Continuing to play spades would have been fatal. You could ill afford to lose a spade as well. It is normally better to attack the suits where your losers are certain and you have no fast winners.*

Suits to leave alone

With high cards spread around the table, it often pays to leave the suit alone. You have a heart stopper, if a defender leads the suit, but you cannot set up a trick yourself. (You would need the A–K in one hand or to hope for a doubleton honor and guess who has it.) If you do not play hearts, maybe a defender will eventually have to.

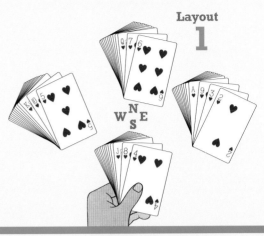

Layout 1

You have one sure winner now, after the ace has gone. Whether you score a second trick depends upon which side leads the suit first. If they do, your eight and nine will force a second trick. If you do, it is either their ten or jack that will become a winner. You would tend to lead this suit only if one winner is enough for your contract.

Layout 2

If you attack the suit, there is little scope for a second trick. You would need someone to hold K–x or Q–x and guess who that is. (Lead low from your hand if West is short or start with the jack if East is). On this entirely normal type of layout, scoring a second winner relies on having the patience to wait for a defender to lead the suit.

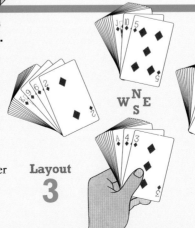

Layout 3

IMPORTANT POINT
On a great many layouts, the side that broaches a suit does so at the cost of a trick. This type of layout is known as a "frozen suit."

Choosing where to win a trick

Both sides vulnerable
Dealer North

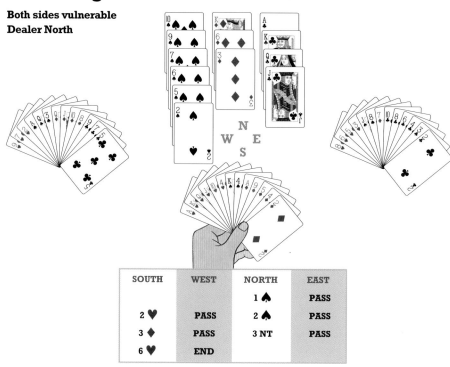

SOUTH	WEST	NORTH	EAST
		1 ♠	PASS
2 ♥	PASS	2 ♠	PASS
3 ♦	PASS	3 NT	PASS
6 ♥	END		

West leads the ♦Q. What is your plan to make this slam contract?

What you know
Barring a six–one trump break, you have 12 top tricks: six trumps, two diamonds, and four clubs. Where you win the first trick depends on your future plan. You want to gain the lead in your hand to draw trumps. You also want to save an entry to dummy for the clubs. On both counts, you want to win the first trick in your hand.

The key plays
1. You should win with the ♦A and lead high trumps.
2. When trumps break four–three, four rounds suffice and you can discard spades from dummy.
3. Next cross to dummy and play four rounds of clubs, discarding four losers. It does not matter that West runs out—she has no trumps left.

IMPORTANT POINT *Had the contract been 6NT by North, declarer could win an opening diamond lead in either hand. The trouble is that West might double to ask East to make an unusual (spade) lead.*

Counting losers

North–South vulnerable
Dealer South

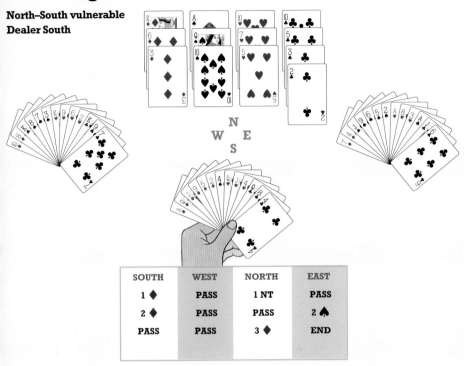

SOUTH	WEST	NORTH	EAST
1 ♦	PASS	1 NT	PASS
2 ♦	PASS	PASS	2 ♠
PASS	PASS	3 ♦	END

West leads the ♠3 and you have a decision to make on the first trick. What are your thoughts?

What you know

You have four certain losers: the ♥A–K and the ♣A–K. You may also have a third club to lose because you could have entry problems even if East holds the A–K. In a contract of 3♦, you cannot afford five losers. To avoid the third club loser you aim to discard a club on a spade.

The key plays

1. Finesse the ♠Q.
2. Draw trumps ending in dummy and discard a club on the ♠A.
3. Continue to play hearts to drive out the A–K and set up a winner.
4. If the contract were 2♦, you would not risk the spade finesse. Instead, you would simply put up the ace, accepting five losers but making sure you do not lose a spade, three clubs, and two hearts.

IMPORTANT POINT *In a suit contract, it is usually a good idea to count losers as well as winners. This will often give you a clue as to how to play.*

Counting shape

North–South vulnerable
Dealer South

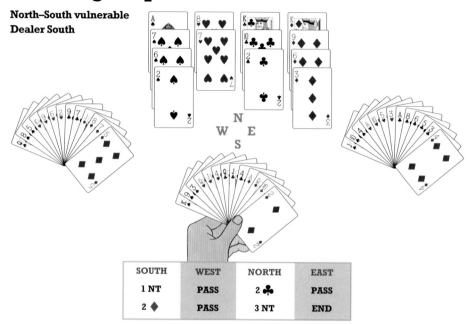

SOUTH	WEST	NORTH	EAST
1 NT	PASS	2 ♣	PASS
2 ♦	PASS	3 NT	END

West leads the ♥2 and the ace wins. East returns the three and you win the third round. How do you play from here?

What you know
The lead and the return both suggest that hearts are four-four, which is good since you are bound to lose a trick to the ♣A. Once that card has gone you will have eight top tricks. The ♦10 or ♦9 will be the ninth. You can cater for J–x–x–x on either side so long as you cash the right top cards first. If you delay the decision until the end of the play, you may know which defender is short.

The key plays
1. You play clubs to knock out the ace.
2. On the fourth round of hearts, you can discard a spade from each hand or a spade from your hand and a club from dummy.
3. Cash your remaining black winners, noting whether all follow to two rounds of spades and three rounds of clubs.
4. When West is short in clubs, cash the ♦A–Q. When East shows out, you have a marked finesse on the third round of diamonds.

IMPORTANT POINT *When you have a choice of ways to play a suit, it is often best to leave it until you have learned more about the hand. A defender short in one suit will tend to have length elsewhere.*

Counting points

North–South vulnerable
Dealer West

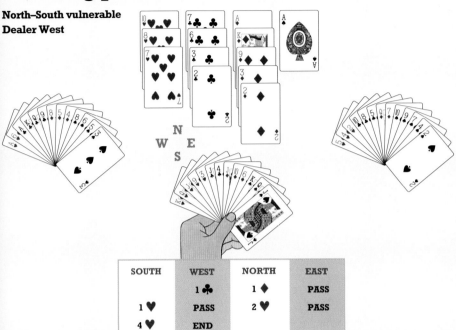

SOUTH	WEST	NORTH	EAST
	1 ♣	1 ♦	PASS
1 ♥	PASS	2 ♥	PASS
4 ♥	END		

West leads the ♣A and continues with the queen and king, East following. What is your plan to make this contract?

What you know

West started with ♣A–K–Q–(x) and since, she opened the bidding, probably the ♥A. If this is not a singleton, she has a balanced hand. This suggests she does not have the right point count to open 1NT. Therefore, she will have only these 13 points if we assume that a 1NT opening would show 15–17.

The key plays

1. You ruff the third club, cash the ♠A, and play trumps.
2. West takes the ace on the first round and plays another club, forcing you to ruff again. You finish drawing trumps.
3. Since West is balanced but did not open 1NT, you place the ♦Q with East and cash the A–K in the hope this card drops. If West had opened 1NT, you would place her with the ♦Q and make the normal play of finessing in diamonds.

IMPORTANT POINT *Count the opposing points, especially if a player has made a limit* *bid or might have done so if holding a particular missing card.*

Inferences

Both sides vulnerable
Dealer East

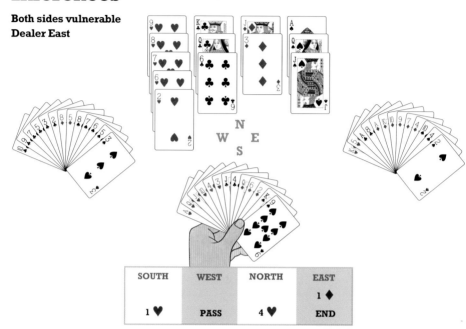

SOUTH	WEST	NORTH	EAST
			1 ♦
1 ♥	PASS	4 ♥	END

West leads the ♦8 and East's king wins. He cashes the ace and plays a third round. West discards a club on this. How do you play from here?

What you know
East started with six diamonds to the A–K. These, together with the ace of clubs, give him enough for an opening bid no matter who has the ♥K. With 11 cards in a suit missing the king, it is usually slightly better to play for the drop than finesse. Here, the fact that West did not ruff the third diamond tips the odds the other way.

The key plays
1. You should work out that, if West held the singleton ♥K, she would have ruffed the third diamond in front of dummy.
2. To get to dummy to finesse in trumps, you ruff your winning ♦Q in dummy (or you can get there with a spade).
3. You then lead a heart to the queen, cash the ace, and claim ten tricks. You lose only a club and the two diamonds already lost.

IMPORTANT POINT *An opponent who fails to ruff one of your winners usually has either a sure trump winner (which you can do nothing about) or no trumps at all.*

Discovery play

Both sides vulnerable
Dealer West

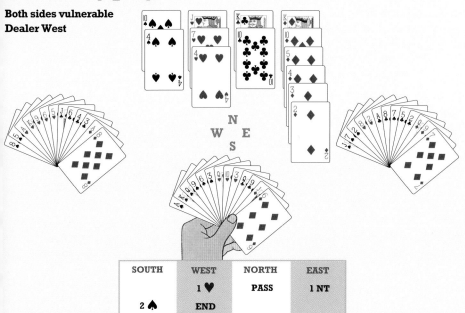

SOUTH	WEST	NORTH	EAST
	1 ♥	PASS	1 NT
2 ♠	END		

West leads the ace, king, and a third heart. East follows twice, ruffs the third round and exits with a trump. What is your plan?

What you know

If West has the ♦A, you want to lead to the king. If West has the ♦Q instead, you want to finesse the ten. You could lead a diamond early to panic West into grabbing the ace if she has it, but relying on this is risky. The bidding suggests that the defenders' 19 points are divided 12–7 or 13–6. Since you have already seen seven from West, whoever has the ♣A is most unlikely to hold the ♦A.

The key plays

1. You draw the missing trumps, which takes only two rounds.
2. You then lead a club to the king and drive out the ♣A.
3. When East has the club ace, you place West with the ♦A to have enough for an opening bid, so you lead to the ♦K.
4. Had West produced the ♣A, you would place East with the ♦A to justify the 1NT response and finesse the ♦10.

IMPORTANT POINT *If the defenders have plenty of values but have not bid, it is a fair bet that their points are evenly split. When* *they have bid, you may be able to place the cards with more certainty.*

Two-way finesses

If you think West has the queen, you usually cash the king and finesse the jack. If you think East does, you usually cash the ace and finesse the ten. You will feel inclined to place West with the queen if you think she has more spades than East or if the bidding marks her with greater overall strength. Ideally, let the opponents lead the suit.

**Layout
2**

You have a two-way finesse again, this time against the jack. You can either finesse the nine (if you think West has it) or the ten (if you think East does). It tends to be harder to place a jack from the bidding, but again it is likely that the defender with more spades has the jack. As before, it would help if the opponents lead the suit.

Guesses are rarely a straight 50–50. Assuming you have no contrary indication, you should tend to play East for the ♥Q. The reason is that if West has Q–9–x–x then you would always have a loser. Thanks to your eight, by leading the ace and continuing with the jack, you can cater for any four-card holding with East.

**Layout
3**

IMPORTANT POINT
It is unusual for a two-way finesse to be a complete guess. Usually the bidding or the distribution provides some clue. If you can, try to arrange for a defender to lead the suit.

King–jack and other guesses

With the K–J facing low cards, you have a choice of plays to score one trick. If you place West with the queen (a safe inference if she leads the suit at trick one against a suit contract), you finesse the jack. If you place West with the ace (perhaps because she does not lead the suit initially) or if you need a trick quickly, put up the king.

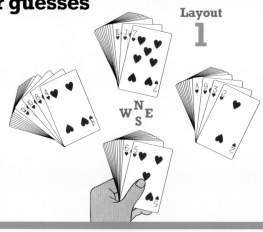

Layout **1**

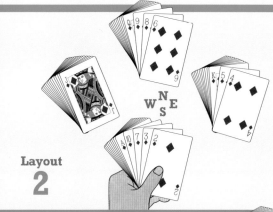

Layout **2**

You need some luck to avoid a loser here. Either East must hold the singleton king (when you cash the ace) or West the singleton jack (when you lead the queen to pin the jack and finesse against the king). Other things being equal, you lead the queen because East may not cover with K–x if he fears that West has the singleton ace.

You might avoid a loser here if West leads the suit. If you place her with the jack, you put in dummy's ten to force out the king. If you think she has the king, go up with the queen. If East has had the chance to lead the suit and has not done so, you would place him with the king and hope that West has the jack.

Layout **3**

IMPORTANT POINT
Always consider what the opponents have not done as well as what they have done. This will often tell you which of two possible layouts is the more likely.

Combining your chances

East–West vulnerable
Dealer North

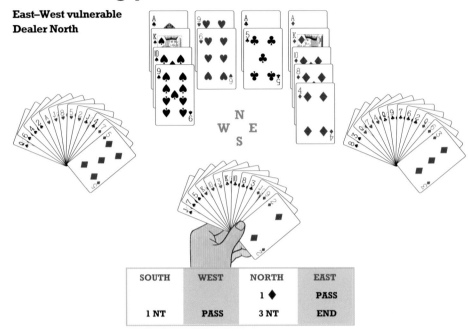

SOUTH	WEST	NORTH	EAST
		1 ♦	PASS
1 NT	PASS	3 NT	END

West leads the ♥5 and East plays the queen. What are your plans here?

What you know
You must win the first trick or risk losing your king. Since the ♥2 and ♥4 are missing, it is likely that the lead comes from a five-card suit. This means that taking a losing finesse will be fatal. With seven top tricks, two more in spades or three more in diamonds will give you your contract. You want to test both suits without losing the lead, giving yourself the best percentage chance of success.

The key plays
1. Having won the heart, cash the ♦A–K. You do this because, with five diamonds and six spades missing, a doubleton queen is more likely in diamonds than in spades.
2. When the queen does not fall, cash the ♠A, come to your hand with a club, and run the ♠J. You can then repeat the spade finesse and arrive at nine tricks.
3. If the ♦Q fell in two rounds, you would not finesse in spades. Instead you would take your ten tricks.

IMPORTANT POINT *If (on a different layout) combining your chances involves losing the lead, it is usually best to test the suit in which you must lose the lead before the potentially running suit.*

Tackling suits in the right order

Both sides vulnerable
Dealer South

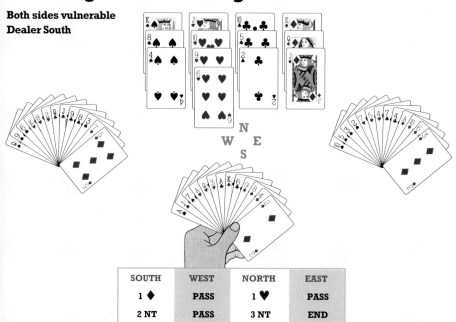

SOUTH	WEST	NORTH	EAST
1 ♦	PASS	1 ♥	PASS
2 NT	PASS	3 NT	END

West leads the ♣Q. How do you plan the play?

What you know

You have five top winners. You might make three more in hearts, two in diamonds, or one in spades. You therefore need to play at least two suits. If East has the ♥K, it will be easy to finesse against it and knock out the ♦A. If the heart finesse is wrong, you need to guard against the danger of losing three club tricks as well. If the lead is from Q–J, West cannot safely continue clubs.

The key plays

1. You should win the first trick to preserve a split tenace in clubs, cross to dummy with the ♠K, and run the ♥J.
2. If West continues clubs, dummy's ten gives you a second stopper; likewise, your ♠J does if she switches to spades.
3. If West exits passively, cash any remaining heart winners in your hand and drive out the ♦A, not caring which defender has it.

IMPORTANT POINT *Even without the ♠J, it would have been right to take the heart finesse. You could afford to lose two spade tricks, which is all you would lose on the normal four–three break.*

Using entries efficiently

Both sides vulnerable
Dealer West

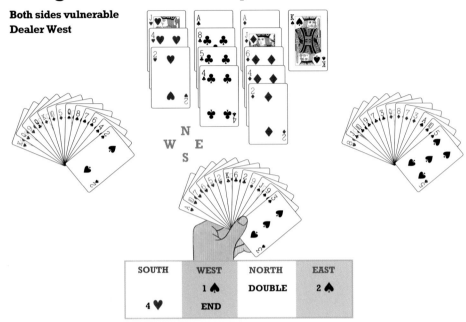

SOUTH	WEST	NORTH	EAST
	1 ♠	DOUBLE	2 ♠
4 ♥	END		

West leads the ♠6 and the ace wins. After a little thought, East switches to the ♣J. What is your plan for ten tricks?

What you know
You have six possible losers: three in spades, two in trumps (on a normal three-one break), and one in clubs. You can ruff two spades in dummy but that still leaves the club loser. On a normal four–three break, you can set up a long diamond by ruffing. You need to take care with entries because you need to ruff three diamonds (unless someone has K–Q–x) and get back to the long diamond.

The key plays
1. Take the ♣K and cash the ♥A.
2. Then, play a diamond to the ace and ruff a diamond.
3. Alternate ruffing spades and diamonds for the next four tricks. If West overruffs, it is with a natural trump winner.
4. Leaving two trumps still out, lead a club. Assuming West does not ruff, take the ace and discard a club on the thirteenth diamond.
5. If West ruffs the second club, she ruffs a loser. Again you lose only two trumps and a spade.

IMPORTANT POINT *If trumps are two-two (40%) and diamonds five–two (30%), an overruff would beat you. The actual distribution of trumps three–one (50%) and diamonds four–three (62%) is much more likely (31% rather than 12%).*

Avoidance play

Both sides vulnerable
Dealer South

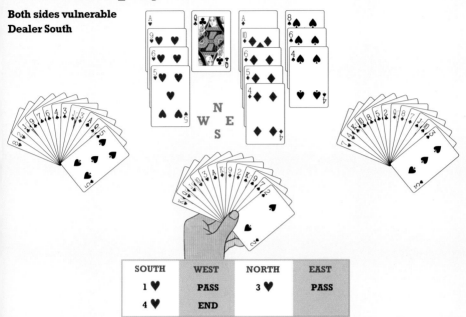

SOUTH	WEST	NORTH	EAST
1 ♥	PASS	3 ♥	PASS
4 ♥	END		

West leads the ♣6 and your ace captures East's king. What is your plan to make this contract?

What you know
You might lose one diamond and, if West has the ♠A, three spades as well. A fourth spade loser is unlikely because you can either ruff it in dummy or discard it on the diamonds. You hope that the diamond suit in dummy will set up to give you two spade discards. The danger to guard against is that, if East gains the lead in diamonds, a spade switch could put you down at once.

The key plays
1. Draw trumps ending in dummy.
2. Then, lead a low diamond off dummy and, as East plays low, play the nine. West wins but cannot profitably attack spades and you are home.
3. If West won with a singleton jack, it would not matter because she would have to return a spade or give you a ruff and discard.
4. If West has Q–J–x–x, you will have a marked finesse on the third round after cashing the king.

IMPORTANT POINT *With a tenace such as K–x or A–Q–x in one hand, you try to lose the lead to the defender who can only lead up to rather than through that holding.*

Morton's Fork

Neither side vulnerable
Dealer South

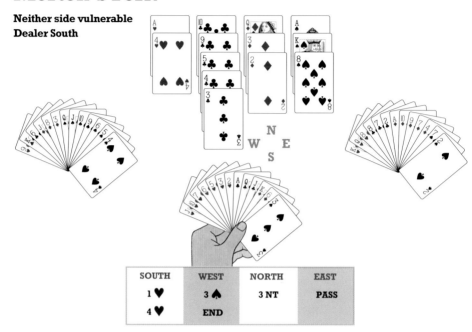

SOUTH	WEST	NORTH	EAST
1 ♥	3 ♠	3 NT	PASS
4 ♥	END		

West leads the ♠Q and dummy's ace wins. What is the safest plan to make this contract?

What you know
If someone (most likely East) has K–Q–x of trumps and West has the king of clubs, you have four losers. You can take one discard on the king of spades but, whether you throw a club or a diamond, you may still have those losers. There is more room for East, who is short in spades, to hold the ♦A. With a type of avoidance play, known as a Morton's Fork, you can turn this to your advantage.

The key plays
1. Lead a low diamond off dummy.
2. If East goes in with the ace and switches to a club, you put up the ace. Then you cash the ♦K, cross to the ♥A and discard two clubs, one on a spade and one on a diamond. You lose two hearts and a diamond, but no clubs.
3. If East lets your ♦K win, simply cross to the ♥A and discard your other diamond on the ♠K. This way you lose two hearts and a club, but no diamonds.

IMPORTANT POINT *With a holding of K–x–x–(x) facing Q–x or similar, it is often good to make the defender you think has the ace play in second seat. Taking the ace then gives you a second trick.*

Deceptive plays

If you expect to lose the lead to West and want to avoid a switch to a different suit, there may be a way to fool her. If she leads the three and East plays the ten, win with the king rather than the jack. The trick will come back if West falls for your ploy and continues spades when she regains the lead.

Layout 1

If you think you can keep West off lead and want to avoid a switch to a different suit, again you can feign weakness. If West leads the jack and East puts up the ace, you drop the queen. Placing you with K–Q doubleton, East will probably return the suit. The trick lost will not come back, so try this only if you have a winner to spare.

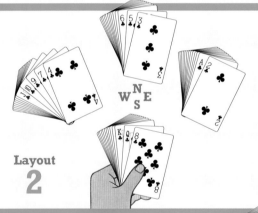

Layout 2

You might also scramble defensive signals with subtle play. If, when West leads the ace and East plays the four, you play the two, West will correctly read East's four as discouraging. If, instead, you play the six, West may think East has played the four from Q–4–2 and continue the suit, setting up your queen.

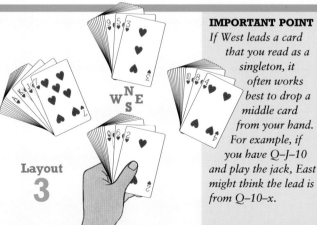

Layout 3

IMPORTANT POINT

If West leads a card that you read as a singleton, it often works best to drop a middle card from your hand. For example, if you have Q–J–10 and play the jack, East might think the lead is from Q–10–x.

PLAY AT NO- TRUMP CONTRACTS

Hold up

Neither side vulnerable
Dealer South

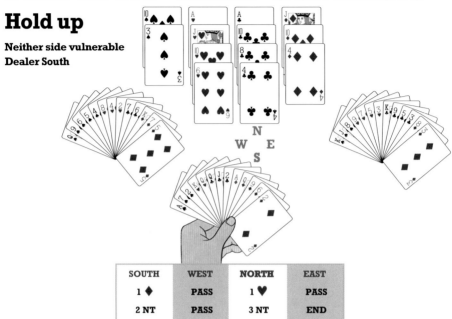

SOUTH	WEST	NORTH	EAST
1 ♦	PASS	1 ♥	PASS
2 NT	PASS	3 NT	END

West leads the ♠5 and East plays the king. What is your plan to make this contract?

What you know
With only seven top tricks (four hearts and three aces), you need two more. Both minors offer sure extra winners once the respective kings have gone and the possibility of running without loss if the finesse works. With the ♠4 missing, there is a danger that West has five spades. You cannot afford to lose four spade tricks and a losing finesse.

The key plays
1. You should duck the first round of spades and East's spade return.
2. Win the third spade and lead the ♣Q for a finesse.
3. If it holds, continue with the jack.
4. If it loses and East can produce a fourth spade, the spades are presumably four–four and you lose only three spades and a club.
5. Do not go to dummy and finesse a diamond into the danger hand.

IMPORTANT POINT *If you placed East with length in spades (if he overcalled perhaps), it would still be correct to hold up.*

In that case, you would take the finesse in diamonds rather than clubs.

Hold up with two stoppers

Both sides vulnerable
Dealer South

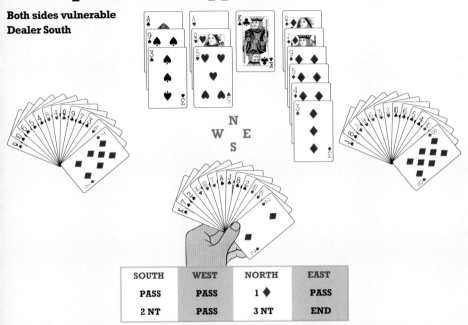

SOUTH	WEST	NORTH	EAST
PASS	PASS	1 ♦	PASS
2 NT	PASS	3 NT	END

West leads the ♠5. What is your plan to make this game?

What you know

You have seven top tricks and it is clear that the extra two must come from diamonds. To set up the suit you need to lose the lead twice. Since the defenders have a head start by leading their long suit, they may be able to run their spades before you can enjoy the diamonds. All will be well if the suit breaks four–three because you can afford to lose two spades. If they are five–two, you need to disrupt their communications.

The key plays

1. You should duck the first trick in both hands, letting the jack win.
2. Win the next spade, in dummy for preference, and lead a diamond.
3. East can win but has no spades left and you win the race.
4. If East had a third spade to lead, spades would be four–three and the contract would not be in danger.
5. It is just too bad if West has five spades and both top diamonds.

IMPORTANT POINT *If you expect to lose the lead twice, you need to take extra care when contemplating a holdup to ensure that any switch is not dangerous. Here you have three heart stoppers and just enough in clubs.*

Preserving a tenace

Both sides vulnerable
Dealer South

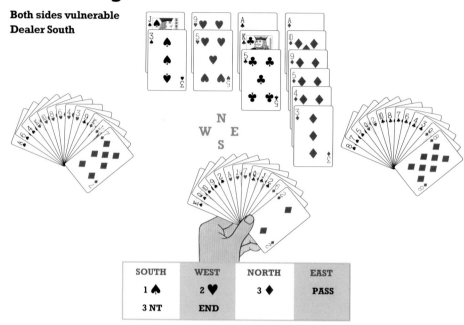

SOUTH	WEST	NORTH	EAST
1 ♠	2 ♥	3 ♦	PASS
3 NT	END		

West leads the ♥3 and, when East plays the queen, you have an early decision to make. What are your thoughts?

What you know
You have five top tricks and, by driving out the ♠A, you will have the four more winners you need. You cannot afford, however, to have the heart suit run against you. You could hold up the ace for two rounds and be sure that East has none left. The snag is that West, who overcalled, is very likely to hold the ♠A. By winning at once, your J–x of hearts will protect you against a lead from West.

The key plays
1. Capture the ♥Q with the ace.
2. Lead your low spade to the jack and continue playing the suit until the ace has gone (leading high might block the suit on a five–one break).
3. If West cashes the ♥K in the hope that your jack is now bare, you will make an overtrick.
4. If West switches to a diamond instead, put up dummy's ace. Then you have nine tricks: four spades, three clubs, and the two red aces.

IMPORTANT POINT *With K–Q–x facing x–x–x (and the ace not played) or A–J–x facing x–x (as here), whether you should win depends on which defender you expect to gain the lead.*

When a switch could be deadly

North–South vulnerable
Dealer South

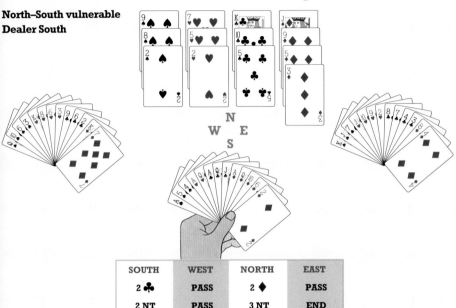

SOUTH	WEST	NORTH	EAST
2 ♣	PASS	2 ♦	PASS
2 NT	PASS	3 NT	END

West leads the ♠3 and East plays the king. How do you assess the situation?

What you know
You have six top tricks and the diamond suit will provide at least three more. Winners are therefore not an issue. With the ♠2 in dummy, the lead of the three marks West with a four- (or three-) card suit. Therefore, you need not worry about the spade suit. You can afford to lose three spades and a diamond. It would be risky to hold up the ♠A because a heart switch could prove fatal.

The key plays
1. Win the first round of spades, capturing the king with the ace.
2. Cross to the ♣K and run the ♦J (or ♦9).
3. If West wins and the defenders cash three more spades, discard the ♥Q from your hand.
4. If, instead, East tries a heart when in with the ♠J, put up the ace. You cannot afford to lose a heart as well as three spades and a diamond.

IMPORTANT POINT *If you thought West had five spades (if the lead was "third and fifth"), you might hold up the ♠A once and cash the ♦A to make sure that West could not get in with a singleton king of diamonds.*

Playing for fast winners

East–West vulnerable
Dealer West

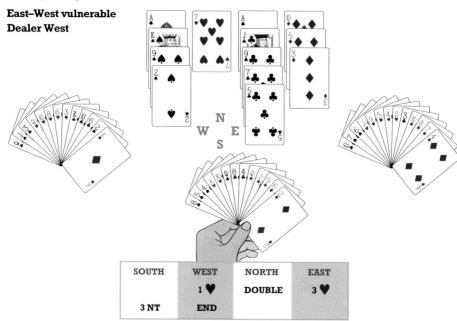

SOUTH	WEST	NORTH	EAST
	1 ♥	DOUBLE	3 ♥
3 NT	END		

West leads the ♥6 and East's jack will lose to your king. What is your plan for nine tricks?

What you know

You have only five top winners. The diamond suit offers the scope for three more winners, but you would still need the club finesse. In any case, by the time you have knocked out two stoppers, the heart suit will be running. Instead, you must play for five club tricks. You could lead low to the jack in case West has K–x or a bare K. However, the combined chance of K–10–x or K–10–x–x is more likely.

The key plays

1. Lead the ♣Q at the second trick.
2. If West covers, win with the ace and exit with a diamond. Win the next heart and run the ♣8, repeating the finesse if need be.
3. If West ducks the first club, you should assume she does not have K–x–x and finesse the nine on the second round. Then exit with a diamond and, upon regaining the lead, finesse the ♣J.

IMPORTANT POINT *Although playing on clubs meant that you needed to find two cards* *well placed, a modest chance is better than no chance at all.*

Knocking out the right stopper first

East–West vulnerable
Dealer West

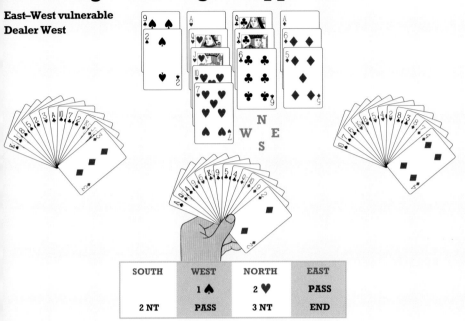

SOUTH	WEST	NORTH	EAST
	1 ♠	2 ♥	PASS
2 NT	PASS	3 NT	END

West leads the ♠5 and East plays the ten. How do you play for the contract?

What you know

You must take the first trick or your ♠Q may never score. Life will be easy if West, who opened the bidding, holds the ♥K. If East has this card, West will have the other missing high cards. Although you cannot hold up on the first trick, you can hold up later. This means you want to knock out West's presumed entry in clubs before doing anything else.

The key plays

1. Take the ♠Q and play a club to the queen.
2. Assuming this holds, continue with the ♣J.
3. When West takes the ♣A and leads a high spade, you duck. Win the third spade and lead the ♥9 for a finesse. East can win but, with no more spades to lead, he cannot harm you.
4. With the ♥K and ♣A gone, you make nine tricks: four hearts, two spades, two clubs, and a diamond.

IMPORTANT POINT *Playing on diamonds would not be good enough even if you guess the suit well. West would clear the spades (knock out your last stopper) and be bound to get in with a club later.*

Blocking the opposing suit

**Both sides vulnerable
Dealer South**

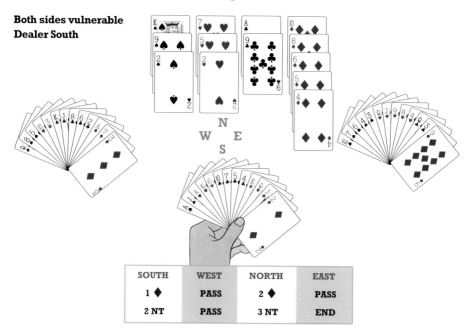

SOUTH	WEST	NORTH	EAST
1 ♦	PASS	2 ♦	PASS
2 NT	PASS	3 NT	END

West leads the ♣6. How do you plan the play?

What you know

You have five top tricks and, by knocking out the ♦A, a clear path to the four more you need. You need to consider the risk of losing four club tricks and a diamond. Holding up the ♣A once will work if West has five clubs and East the ♦A. It is better, however, to win the first club since West would hardly lead low from K–Q–J–x–x. If East has a doubleton honor, the suit will be blocked.

The key plays

1. Put up dummy's ♣A on the first trick.
2. Lead a low diamond to the king and continue playing the suit until the ace has gone.
3. If East unblocked the ♣Q at trick one, or if West plays the ♣K next, your ten will be good on the fourth round.
4. If not, the defenders can cash only one club trick before you get in.
5. With the ♦A gone, you have nine tricks and so will not risk leading a spade to the jack.

IMPORTANT POINT *With A–x facing 10–x–x–x (no nine in either hand), you still put up the ace if you think West will gain the lead. Only if East has an entry and knows to unblock, is it better to hold up.*

Playing a short suit

East–West vulnerable
Dealer North

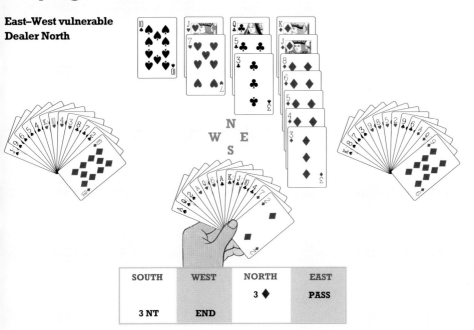

SOUTH	WEST	NORTH	EAST
		3 ♦	PASS
3 NT	END		

West leads the ♠5 and East plays the king. How do you plan the play?

What you know

After the play so far, you have eight top tricks. You can potentially make a lot of extra winners in diamonds. The snag is that you cannot be sure of any. If spades are five–four (likely), you can afford to lose the lead only once, so losing the ♦J to the queen or the ♦K to the ace will leave you dependent on the heart finesse. By contrast, if you play hearts, you will set up a winner even if the finesse loses.

The key plays

1. Duck the first trick (in case East helpfully switches to a heart).
2. Win the second spade, cross to the ♣Q (perhaps after cashing the ace first), and lead the ♥J for a finesse.
3. When West wins and clears the spades, take your nine tricks: two spades, two hearts, and five clubs.
4. If East had the king of hearts, he would cover the jack and you could try diamonds for an overtrick.

IMPORTANT POINT *At matchpoint pairs, it would be reasonable to play diamonds before hearts. The chance of overtrick(s) justifies risking a normal contract.*

PLAY AT SUIT CONTRACTS

Ruffs in dummy

You can take four heart ruffs, generating four winners, if dummy has enough spare trumps and you have enough entries to your hand. The fact that a short side suit translates into tricks explains why, in the bidding, you can count short suits as an asset.

This is a more typical layout. After cashing the ace, there is a good chance that you can ruff one heart in dummy, come back to your hand in another suit, and ruff a second heart. This gives you two tricks that you could not score in a no-trump contract. This heart suit and the one above would be liabilities in a no-trump contract.

Layout
2

You could ruff either the third or the fourth round. Normally it is best to cash two winners only and then ruff the third round. This protects your high cards against an opposing ruff on a five–two break. It tends to be better to try to cash all three winners only if you cannot draw trumps after taking the ruff.

Layout
3

IMPORTANT POINT
Whenever dummy first appears, look to see if it has any side suits shorter than your own—these represent a possible source of ruffing winners in a suit contract.

Setting up ruffs

To score two ruffs you first give up a spade. The defenders, seeing you play dummy's short suit, will probably switch to trumps. You will therefore tend to need at least three trumps in dummy to be able to score two ruffs. You will also need at least one quick reentry so that you can get back to your hand after taking the first spade ruff.

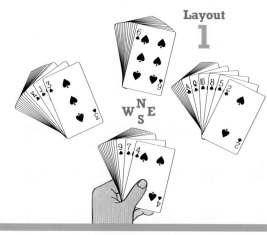

Layout
1

Layout
2

To set up one ruff you should normally duck the first round. In comparison to playing ace and another, this has two advantages. First, your ace provides a ready-made entry for taking a ruff. Second, if the defenders are able to remove dummy's trumps, your ace leaves you with some control over the suit.

It can be hard work to set up a ruff. To ruff the fourth round of hearts (when the suits fails to split three–three) you must lose the lead twice and get back to your hand to play the fourth round. Holding back the ace is not a good idea with this layout because, if the suit is not three–three, one opponent will be shorter than dummy.

Layout
3

Drawing trumps

Neither side vulnerable
Dealer South

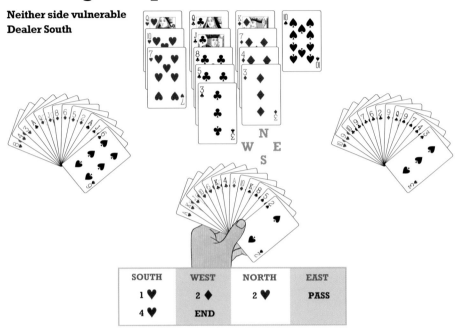

SOUTH	WEST	NORTH	EAST
1 ♥	2 ♦	2 ♥	PASS
4 ♥	END		

West leads the ♣A and switches to the ♦Q. What is the safest plan for this contract?

What you know

You have ten tricks: five hearts, three clubs, and two diamonds. So, you do not need to ruff any spades in dummy. The danger in attempting to take ruffs is that West can ruff clubs and East diamonds. With five trumps missing, they will split either three–two, four–one or five–zero. Noting when one defender shows out is an easier way to work out whether you have drawn them rather than counting every card.

The key plays

1. You should win the second trick in your hand and lead a low trump.
2. Win in dummy, cash dummy's other high trump, and lead a trump to your hand. Since everyone followed for two rounds, the suit was three–two and you can stop drawing trumps.
3. So cash the ♣K, cross to the ♦K (this is why you won trick two in your hand), and cash the ♣Q–J.
4. Having discarded two spades on the clubs, you can now lead to the ♠K for a possible overtrick.

IMPORTANT POINT *Drawing trumps is wise either if you have enough tricks for your contract without taking ruffs or if dummy will still have enough trumps left for ruffing after you have drawn the opposing trumps.*

Leaving one trump out

Both sides vulnerable
Dealer North

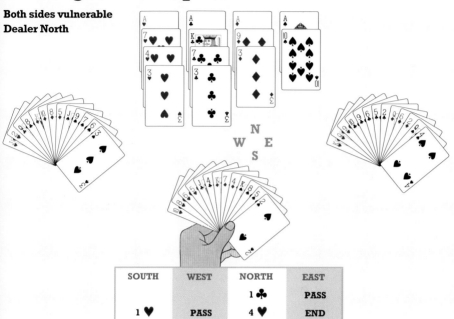

SOUTH	WEST	NORTH	EAST
		1 ♣	PASS
1 ♥	PASS	4 ♥	END

West leads the ♦J. What is your plan to make this game contract?

The key plays
1. Win the diamond in either hand and duck the first round of trumps. The point of this is that you want to draw exactly two rounds of trumps.
2. Win the return, cash the ace of trumps, and cash your other side winners.
3. Ruff spades in dummy and clubs in your hand, not caring if someone overruffs. The missing trump is a winner anyway and you need only three out of the four ruffs to generate an extra trick.

What you know
You have seven top tricks. Unless you decide to lead up to the ♣J and find East with the queen, trumps will need to provide the other three you need. If you draw three rounds of trumps, you can make the remaining one in each hand independently, but that gives you only two extra tricks. You might make more ruffing winners if you draw no trumps, but a defender with two trumps might overruff you.

IMPORTANT POINT *It is often a good idea to leave a master trump out rather than* *expending a trump in both your own hand and dummy's to draw it.*

Taking a quick discard

East–West vulnerable
Dealer South

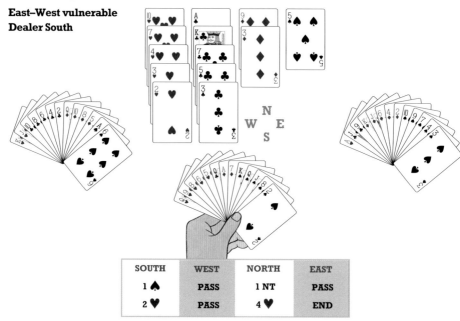

SOUTH	WEST	NORTH	EAST
1 ♠	PASS	1 NT	PASS
2 ♥	PASS	4 ♥	END

West leads the ♦5. What is your plan on this deal?

What you know

After the lead, you have four top losers: the ace–king of hearts, the ♠A, and a diamond. You cannot do anything about the first three losers, so you must avoid losing a diamond. It is no good playing to discard a diamond from dummy on a spade. As soon as you lose the lead, the defenders will cash their winner. You must discard a diamond from your hand even though it means overtaking the queen of clubs.

The key plays

1. Take the ♦A.
2. Lead the ♣Q to the ace.
3. Continue with the ♣K, discarding a diamond.
4. Now is the time to play trumps. You do not want to give East the chance to ruff a club with a singleton ace or king of trumps.
5. At leisure, you can knock out the ♠A and score ten tricks. Any spades that are not winners you ruff in dummy.

IMPORTANT POINT *You cannot ignore fast losers that mean you will be down as soon as you lose the lead. You must try to dispose of your excess losers first.*

Trumps as entries

North–South vulnerable
Dealer South

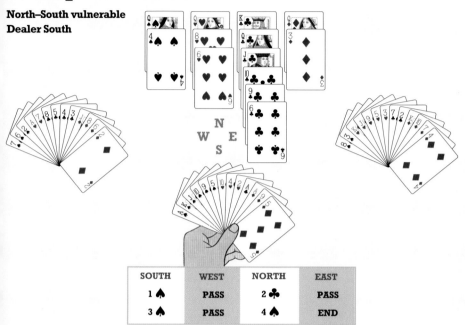

SOUTH	WEST	NORTH	EAST
1 ♠	PASS	2 ♣	PASS
3 ♠	PASS	4 ♠	END

West leads the ♦2. You try dummy's queen but East produces the king. How should you plan the play?

What you know

You have three possible heart losers and two possible diamond losers. Ruffing a diamond in dummy would sort out only one of these. The long club suit is your best bet. The question is how many trumps to draw. Taking three rounds is clearly no good because then you can never get back to dummy. The correct technique is to take two rounds only. A defender with two–two in the black suits cannot then ruff.

The key plays

1. Win the first diamond and cash the ♣A.
2. Cash the ♠A and cross to dummy with the queen.
3. Lead clubs from dummy, discarding diamonds from your hand. You will be able to take the discards you need if either the clubs break three–three or the defender with short clubs has no more than two trumps.
4. As the cards lie, you discard three losers and make an overtrick.

IMPORTANT POINT *Entries are critical to the play of many contracts. Do not draw all the trumps if you need one or more early trump winners as entries.*

Not ruffing in the long hand

East–West vulnerable
Dealer South

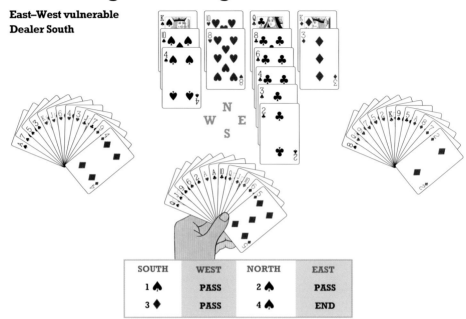

SOUTH	WEST	NORTH	EAST
1 ♠	PASS	2 ♠	PASS
3 ♦	PASS	4 ♠	END

West leads the ♥4 and you will take East's queen with your ace. What is the safest plan for ten tricks?

What you know

On the face of it, you have only three losers: the ♠A, a diamond, and a club. The main danger is a four–one trump break, which occurs 28% of the time. You will have to lose the lead twice and you cannot afford to ruff twice in the long trump hand if the trumps break four–one. To avoid being forced twice, you will need to use dummy's trumps to help you deal with heart leads.

The key plays

1. Play a trump to the king and a low one back to your queen.
2. If West correctly ducks these two tricks, you abandon trumps. Play diamonds next, driving out the ace.
3. When East returns a heart, do not ruff. Discard the ♣10 instead—it is a loser anyway. If the defenders play a third round of hearts, dummy can ruff. You then drive out the ♠A and draw trumps.

IMPORTANT POINT *Ruffing in the long trump hand, except for the purpose of setting up a suit in dummy or removing the defenders' exit cards, is something to avoid if you possibly can.*

Holding the lead

East–West vulnerable
Dealer South

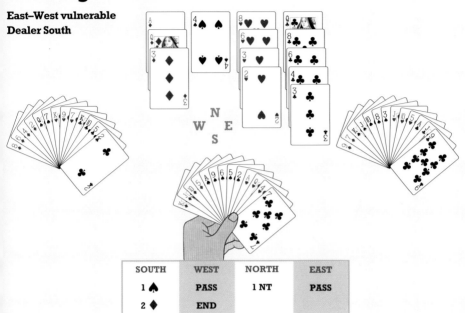

SOUTH	WEST	NORTH	EAST
1 ♠	PASS	1 NT	PASS
2 ♦	END		

West leads the ♦2. How do you play for the contract?

What you know

You have many potential losers, so this time it seems easier to count winners. Four diamond tricks and the two major-suit aces give you six. Setting up a long spade would involve a lot of hard work, so the realistic chances for extra winners are spade ruffs or the heart finesse. Indeed, if you can make four trump tricks and take two ruffs, you need not risk the heart finesse.

The key plays

1. Win the first trick in dummy—you do not want to ruff high twice in dummy because your ♦5 could then be a loser.
2. Play a spade to the ace and ruff a spade.
3. Next, play a heart to the ace, spurning the finesse. For fear of a trump continuation, you cannot afford to lose the lead, either to the ♥K or by giving up a club.
4. Finally, ruff a second spade in dummy to ensure your eighth trick.

IMPORTANT POINT *On this auction you expected West's trump lead. North, to leave* *you in your second suit, is clearly short in your first suit, spades.*

Ruffing finesse

You can choose who to play for the king. If you think West has it, you take a simple finesse. In a suit contract, you have another option: cash the ace and lead the queen, planning to run it if not covered. If East covers, you ruff and return to dummy to take a discard on the jack. Even if West has the king, at least you have thrown out one loser.

Layout
1

Layout
2

The void makes up for missing the ace. Lead the king and keep playing hearts until East plays the ace. When he does, you ruff. Your trump is like a super ace and lets you (with the help of the four–four break), make four heart tricks without losing any. If West had the ace, you might still make four tricks but you would lose one on the way.

A double ruffing finesse may be possible when there are two key cards missing. Lead the queen, discarding a loser and allowing West to take the ace. Later you lead the jack for a simple ruffing finesse against the king. If East had both the ace and the king, you would ruff each time he covers and make a diamond without losing the lead.

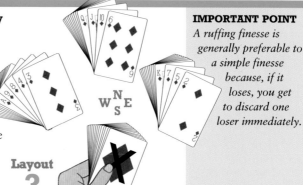

Layout
3

IMPORTANT POINT
A ruffing finesse is generally preferable to a simple finesse because, if it loses, you get to discard one loser immediately.

Setting up a suit

Both sides vulnerable
Dealer South

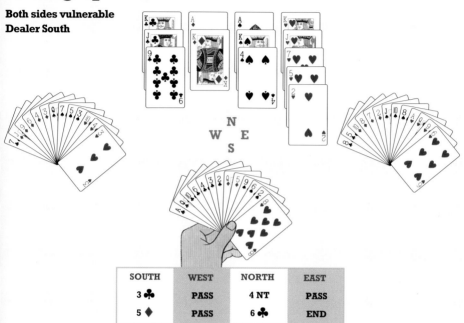

SOUTH	WEST	NORTH	EAST
3 ♣	PASS	4 NT	PASS
5 ♦	PASS	6 ♣	END

West leads the ♦4. What is your plan?

What you know

You have a quick heart loser (unless West has the ace and ducks it) and a slow spade loser. You have a chance of discarding a spade on a heart via a winning guess in hearts (or if West has the ace–queen). Even if that does not work, you should be able to set up a long heart on the normal four–three break. You will need to ruff three hearts and get back to the long heart. Fortunately, dummy contains plenty of entries.

The key plays

1. Draw two rounds of trumps, ending in your hand, and lead a heart.
2. When West plays low, you try the jack but East wins with the queen.
3. Win the return in dummy and ruff a heart to your hand.
4. Using two more entries to dummy (it is best to save a spade until last in case you need a squeeze), ruff two more hearts in your hand.
5. Finally, cross back to dummy to cash the thirteenth heart.

IMPORTANT POINT *Given sufficient entries in one hand and trumps in the other, you can set up any suit in which one of you has greater length than either defender.*

Ruffing down a high card

Declarer can make a heart trick by reading the position. If East has bid the suit, and West has raised, you can picture this type of layout. Play low on West's lead of the six and East's jack will win. Later, you ruff a low heart and then lead the king to pin West's queen and ruff out East's ace. This sets up the ten as a fourth-round winner.

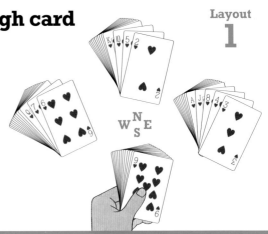

Layout **1**

With no clue from the bidding, the normal play is to cash the ace and twice lead low from dummy, ruffing each time. You hope that the king is with a doubleton or three-card suit. You might play differently if East had bid the suit. Then you might lead the queen on the second or third round, playing West for three to the jack.

Layout **2**

You could take a finesse against the queen, and that is the normal play in the suit. Suppose, however, that you are only playing this suit as an extra chance (like the diamond suit on page 162). In this case, it may be better to play ace, king, and ruff. If the queen falls, fine. If not, you still have the lead and can try your luck elsewhere.

Layout **3**

IMPORTANT POINT

If you stop to think about the bidding or a defender's opening lead, you will often be able to guess who has the length or strength in a suit—this will help you decide how to play it.

Ruffing entries

**Neither side vulnerable
Dealer South**

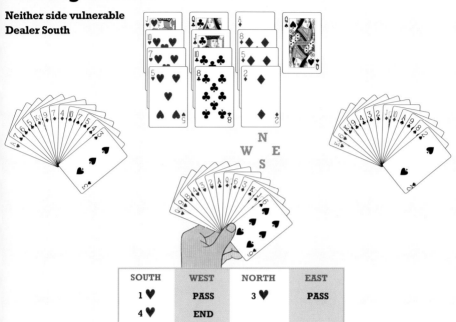

SOUTH	WEST	NORTH	EAST
1 ♥	PASS	3 ♥	PASS
4 ♥	END		

West leads the ♠4. East wins with the ace and switches to the ♦J. What is the best plan for this contract?

What you know

If the ♦Q holds, you can simply discard two diamonds from dummy on your spades. If West covers with the king, you will have to win and face the prospect of five top losers. Two discards in your spades will be no good and you must instead try to do something with dummy's clubs. You will need a successful ruffing finesse and two fast entries to dummy.

The key plays

1. Cover with the ♦Q and, when West plays the ♦K, win in dummy.
2. Unblock the ♣A and ruff a winning spade in dummy.
3. Lead a club from dummy, planning to discard a diamond if the king does not appear but ruffing when it does.
4. Ruff another winning spade and discard your remaining diamonds on the clubs. Clubs do not break four–four, but West can only ruff high. You lose two trumps and the ♠A, but nothing else.

IMPORTANT POINT *An alternative strategy is to try to crash the ace and king of trumps on the same trick. If West is a weak player* *and holds K–x, leading low from your hand might work.*

Combating defensive ruffs

Neither side vulnerable
Dealer South

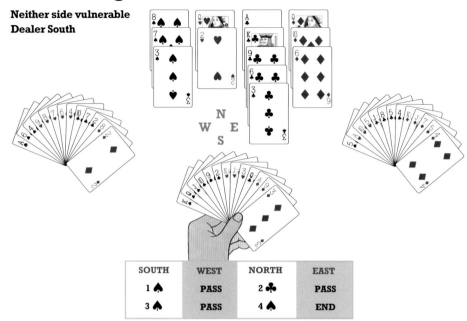

SOUTH	WEST	NORTH	EAST
1 ♠	PASS	2 ♣	PASS
3 ♠	PASS	4 ♠	END

West leads the ♦8. What is the safest line for this game contract?

What you know

The lead cannot be fourth highest, so it looks like East has the ♦K and ♦J. You therefore have one diamond and two aces to lose. There is also the danger, especially if East–West do not use old-fashioned "top-of-nothing" leads, of incurring a ruff. With two aces missing, the chance of keeping East off the play is not high. A better bet is to find a way to use dummy's high clubs and your good trumps.

The key plays

1. Play the ♦Q from dummy and capture the king with the ace.
2. Lead the ♣Q and overtake in dummy. After that, cash a second club, discarding a diamond.
3. Lead a high trump from dummy and continue leading the suit to drive out the ace.
4. If East then gets in with the ♦J and plays a third round of diamonds, ruff high.
5. After drawing trumps, you can knock out the ♥A at leisure.

IMPORTANT POINT *If the club suit did not offer a quick discard, your best bet would be to duck the first diamond. A five–two break is much more likely than a six–one break and West could hold both missing aces.*

Scissors coup

Both sides vulnerable
Dealer West

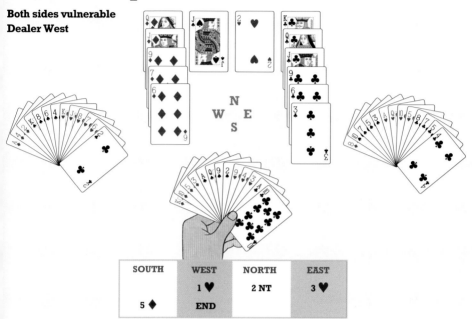

SOUTH	WEST	NORTH	EAST
	1 ♥	2 NT	3 ♥
5 ♦	END		

West leads the ♣2. What is your plan on this deal?

What you know

You have two certain losers, the red aces. The opening lead also seems ominous. Since you can see all the club honors, it looks like West has a singleton. Presumably she plans to win the first trump, put East in with a heart, and receive a club ruff. To avoid this you must dispose of dummy's heart. Finessing the ♠Q is an option but West, who opened the bidding, probably has the king.

The key plays

1. Win the first club in dummy and lead the ♠J.
2. When East plays low, overtake with the ace and return the queen.
3. West covers and you discard a heart from dummy. By swapping a heart loser for a spade loser you do not gain a trick directly but you do prevent East from getting the lead unless he has the trump ace.
4. Upon regaining the lead, you draw trumps, knocking out the ace.

IMPORTANT POINT *A lead in an unexpected suit, especially if it is a small card* *and you can see most or all of the honors in the suit, is often a singleton.*

Dummy reversal

East–West vulnerable
Dealer South

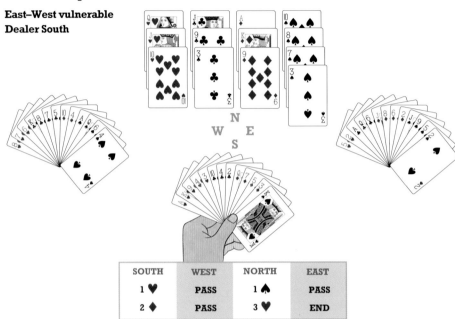

SOUTH	WEST	NORTH	EAST
1 ♥	PASS	1 ♠	PASS
2 ♦	PASS	3 ♥	END

West leads the ♣5 and the ace wins.
A spade switch goes to the ace and West shifts to a trump. How do you play?

What you know

With four top losers in the black suits, you cannot lose a diamond. What can you do if diamonds are not three–three? One idea is to draw two rounds of trumps, hoping that the defender short in diamonds is also short in trumps. Then you could ruff the fourth round. Another plan is to ruff three spades in your hand. Assuming you do not run into a ruff, you will just need a three–two trump split. This offers better odds.

The key plays

1. Win the trump in dummy and ruff a spade high.
2. Cross back to dummy with a trump and, when all follow again, ruff a second spade high.
3. Cross again to dummy with a diamond and ruff a third spade high.
4. Cross back to dummy with a diamond and draw the last trump.
5. You can now cash the ♦Q and possibly (if the suit breaks three–three) a long diamond as well.

IMPORTANT POINT *You ruffed the spades high because you needed trump entries to dummy. You used those entries before the* *diamonds to give yourself the option to stop ruffing if trumps broke four–one.*

Avoiding an overruff

East–West vulnerable
Dealer North

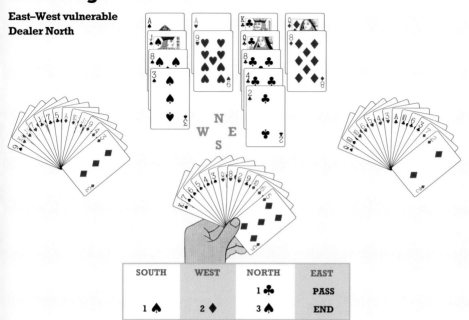

SOUTH	WEST	NORTH	EAST
		1 ♣	PASS
1 ♠	2 ♦	3 ♠	END

West leads the ♦A–K, on which East plays high-low, and continues with the jack. How do you play this part-score?

What you know

Given West's overcall and East's encouraging high-low signal, you can be sure that East has no more diamonds. One way to stop East from overruffing is to ruff with the ace. However, unless the queen of trumps is bare or West has the ♣A, you will lose one trick in each suit to add to the two diamonds already lost. Rather than ruffing a diamond, it is better to ruff a heart, a suit East cannot overruff.

The key plays

1. Discard a heart from dummy on the third round of diamonds.
2. Win West's probable heart switch with dummy's now singleton ace.
3. Play a spade to the king (in case East is void) and one back to the ace to finish drawing trumps.
4. Lead the ♣K from dummy to drive out the ace.
5. Ruff one heart in dummy and throw the other on a top club.

IMPORTANT POINT *Discard a loser so that you can ruff a different suit can be equally useful when a ruff in the long trump hand might be overruffed.*

Ruffing high

East–West vulnerable
Dealer South

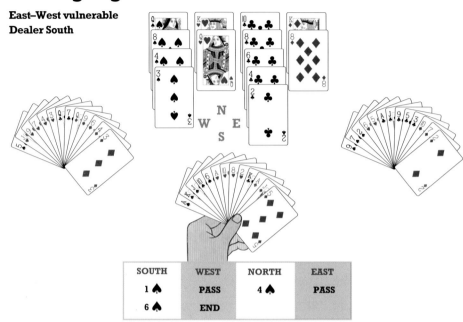

SOUTH	WEST	NORTH	EAST
1 ♠	PASS	4 ♠	PASS
6 ♠	END		

West leads the ♥4. How do you play this slam?

What you know
You have ten sure tricks: five trumps, three hearts, and two diamonds. If the ♥J falls in three rounds, the ♥10 will be a winner, while the ♦J might be if you successfully finesse East for the ♦Q. On a four–three break, you might also be able to set up a long club. However, the safer way to generate extra winners is to ruff red losers in dummy. You can afford to ruff one with the eight and the other with the queen.

The key plays
1. Lead a club and win the probable heart return. (You want to set up a quick route to your hand to avoid a possible fourth-round heart ruff.)
2. After cashing one high trump, play a diamond to the king, one back to the ace, and ruff the third round with the ♠8.
3. Return to your hand with a trump and ruff the ♥10 with ♠Q. East is out of hearts but obviously he cannot overruff.
4. Ruff a club to your hand and draw the missing trumps.

IMPORTANT POINT *A six–two diamond break is less likely than a five–two heart break, which is why you ruffed the diamond with the eight. You had to do that first so that East could not discard a diamond on the third heart and then overruff.*

Cross-ruff

East–West vulnerable
Dealer South

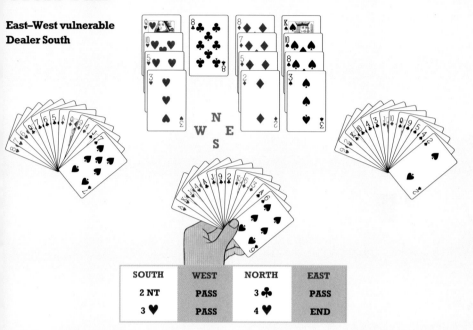

SOUTH	WEST	NORTH	EAST
2 NT	PASS	3 ♣	PASS
3 ♥	PASS	4 ♥	END

West leads the ♥7. What is the best plan for ten tricks?

What you know

On this deal, again it looks easier to count winners than losers. You have three top winners in the side suits, four certain trump winners, and the possibility of scoring the ♦K. Therefore, since the ♣J and ♠10 are unlikely to score, you will need at least two and preferably three ruffs. A five–two spade break is more likely than a seven–one or six–two club break, so you want to ruff spades high if you can.

The key plays

1. Win the first trump in dummy, disposing of the only low trump in your hand.
2. Play a spade to the ace and one back to the king.
3. Then, play a club to the ace and ruff a club low.
4. Ruff a spade (high) and ruff another club low.
5. You now have only high trumps in each hand and can ruff a second spade and a third club without fear of an overruff.

IMPORTANT POINT *Taking a club ruff or two before ruffing any spades would also work. The important part of the timing was* *making sure you could ruff three clubs without losing the lead.*

ENDGAME STRATEGY

Avoiding a guess

East–West vulnerable
Dealer South

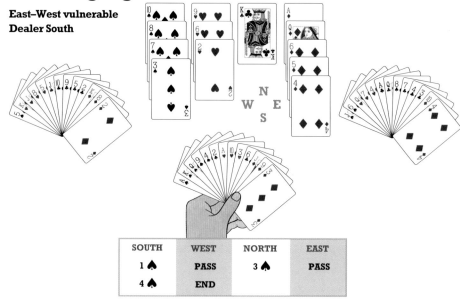

SOUTH	WEST	NORTH	EAST
1 ♠	PASS	3 ♠	PASS
4 ♠	END		

West leads the ♣J, which East wins with the ace. He switches to the ♥4, which makes it look as if the hearts are four–three. What is the best way to handle this contract?

What you know
Losing a diamond would be fatal, so you need West to hold the king. What do you do, though, if all follow low as you finesse the queen? Do you cash the ace, playing West for K–x, or do you come to your hand and lead the jack, playing East for 10–x? To resolve this, do neither; instead, force the opponents to lead the second round of diamonds.

The key plays
1. Win the second round of hearts, draw trumps in two rounds, finesse the ♦Q, and exit with a heart.
2. If West leads any diamond or East leads the ten, life is easy.
3. If East wins and leads a low diamond (not that he can), try putting in the nine.
4. If East wins and leads a club (as could happen if West holds ♦K–10–x–x), discard a diamond and ruff in dummy.

IMPORTANT POINT *Suits you want to make the opponents lead to save you a guess include any with a two-way finesse: A–J–x facing K–10–x, Q–9–x facing K–10–x and Q–9–x facing J–8–x.*

Getting a lead into a tenace

Both sides vulnerable
Dealer West

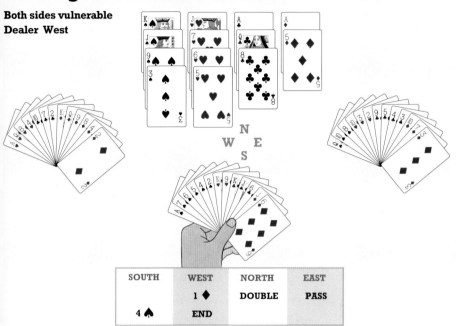

SOUTH	WEST	NORTH	EAST
	1 ♦	DOUBLE	PASS
4 ♠	END		

West leads the ♦K. What is your plan for ten tricks?

What you know

You have one diamond loser, two heart losers (West is likely to have the ace to open the bidding), and a possible trump loser if West is void (you can finesse if East is void). Since West must have the ♦Q on the lead, your ♦J gives you a sure way of making her play. If her only options then are to lead a heart or give you a ruff and discard, the contract will definitely make.

The key plays

1. Take the ♦A and lead a trump to the ace.
2. Noting that West shows out, play a trump back to the king and then take three rounds of clubs.
3. When East cannot ruff, lead (or lead up to) the ♦J.
4. If West, after winning, leads a minor-suit card, ruff in dummy and discard a heart from your hand. A heart switch would also suit you fine.

IMPORTANT POINT *If you had the ♥K in dummy (and West had not bid), you would duck the first trick and aim to put East in with his trump trick to make him open up the hearts.*

The frozen suit

East–West vulnerable
Dealer East

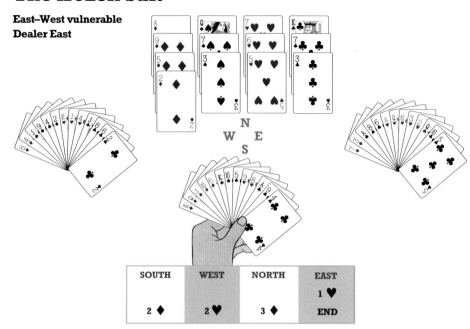

SOUTH	WEST	NORTH	EAST
			1 ♥
2 ♦	2 ♥	3 ♦	END

West leads the ♥4. East wins with the ace and switches to the ♣5. What is your plan on this deal?

What you know

You have four certain losers—two hearts, a club, and the ♠A. You therefore need to avoid losing to the ♠J. This will be easy if East has it. Also, a spade lead from either of the defenders will do the trick. East, who does not seem to have the ♥K or too much in clubs, needs the ♠A for his opening bid. To force a spade return, you must first strip the hearts.

The key plays

1. Win the club in either hand, cash two trumps, and give up a heart.
2. Win the next club, go to dummy with a trump (if there are any out or you are not there already), ruff a heart, and give up a club.
3. If West wins and leads a spade, you have a free finesse.
4. If East wins and leads a spade, the ♠K and ♠Q will both score.
5. A ruff and discard is equally helpful and you can ruff in either hand.

IMPORTANT POINT *Remember, this spade position is called a "frozen suit" and is an ideal layout to force the opponents to lead. For more examples, see page 153.*

The evenly divided suit

North–South vulnerable
Dealer East

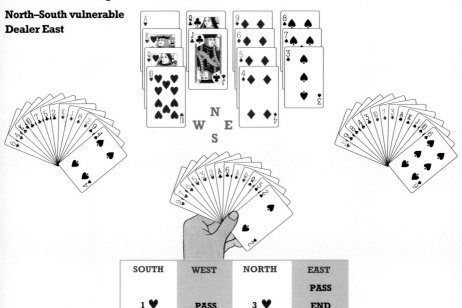

SOUTH	WEST	NORTH	EAST
			PASS
1 ♥	PASS	3 ♥	END

West leads the ♠9. East cashes the king and ace and plays a third round. West ruffs and exits with a trump. What is your plan?

What you know

East, who passed as dealer, can hardly have a king anywhere as well as ♠A–K–J–10–x. A finesse in either minor is thus doomed to failure. You need to throw West in to force her to lead into a tenace. You already know she cannot exit in spades and can easily draw trumps, so she will have no easy exit cards. The important thing is to make sure that she cannot play back the suit you use to throw her in.

The key plays

1. Note that East follows to the first trump so that trumps are drawn.
2. Play a club to the ace and lead a second round of clubs.
3. West wins and must either lead a diamond into your A–Q or lead a club. In the latter case, dummy ruffs and you discard the ♦Q.
4. If you mistakenly played ace and another diamond, West would win and exit in diamonds, leaving you to play clubs yourself.

IMPORTANT POINT *A suit in which you and dummy have the same length (here clubs) is good as an exit suit. On occasion, you can discard from one hand to set up an evenly divided suit with which to exit.*

Loser on loser as an exit

**East–West vulnerable
Dealer South**

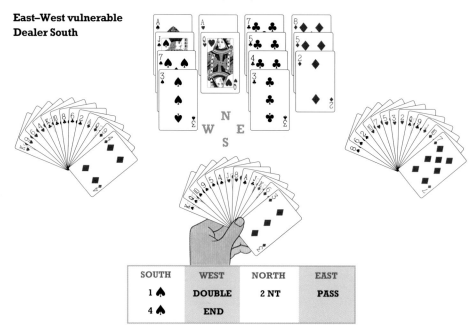

SOUTH	WEST	NORTH	EAST
1 ♠	DOUBLE	2 NT	PASS
4 ♠	END		

West leads the ♣6 and East plays the queen. What is the best plan for ten tricks?

What you know
The heart finesse should work but no doubt West, who made the take-out double, has the ♦A as well. Unless she has something like A–Q–J–10 or A–Q–J–10–9, it will not be possible to duck a diamond into her hand. If you want to force her to lead the suit, you need to throw her in with a club. This should work whenever she has club length because you will simply be losing a club more and a diamond less.

The key plays
1. Take the first club, draw trumps, and give up a club.
2. West does best to play a heart and you finesse the queen.
3. After that, ruff a club, go over to the ♥A, and throw a diamond on the fourth round of clubs.
4. If West leads a club or a heart next, you can ruff in dummy and throw a diamond from your hand. If she leads a diamond, your king scores.

IMPORTANT POINT *A loser on loser play can be a good way to achieve a throw in* *when you have several losers in the suit you want your opponent to lead.*

Obtaining a ruff and discard

Both sides vulnerable
Dealer West

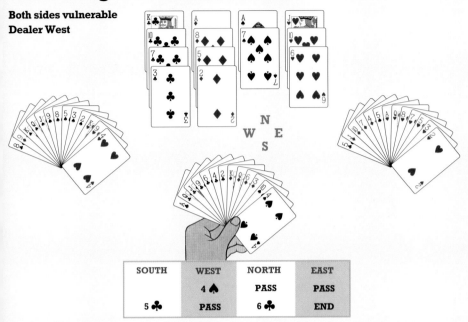

SOUTH	WEST	NORTH	EAST
	4 ♠	PASS	PASS
5 ♣	PASS	6 ♣	END

West leads the ♠K. How do you play for this slam?

What you know

You have a spade loser exposed by the lead and potentially a slow diamond loser. Given West's spade length, East is much more likely than West to hold four diamonds. If East has A–K–Q of hearts, you can squeeze him, but this is uncertain. A better plan is to strip the hearts, planning to put West in with the second round of spades to give you a ruff and discard.

The key plays

1. Win the spade and ruff a heart immediately.
2. Go to dummy with a trump and ruff a second heart.
3. Go back to dummy with a trump and ruff a third round of hearts.
4. Cash two top diamonds and, when West shows out, lead a spade.
5. With only spades left, West must return the suit. You ruff in one hand and discard a diamond from the other.

IMPORTANT POINT *As the cards lie (with spades eight–one) you could also succeed by putting East in with the fourth round of diamonds. A ruff and discard from him would allow you to avoid a spade loser.*

Partial elimination

Both sides vulnerable
Dealer East

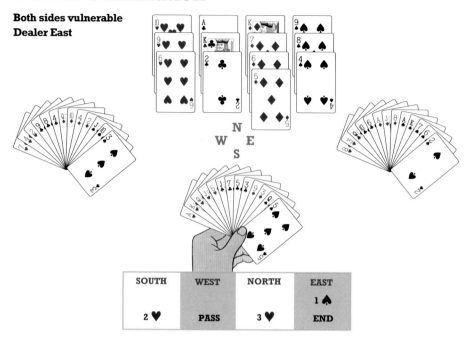

SOUTH	WEST	NORTH	EAST
			1 ♠
2 ♥	PASS	3 ♥	END

West leads the ♠J. East plays two top spades and a third round. You ruff high and West drops the ten. How do you play from here?

What you know
You cannot afford to lose two diamonds and a club. Sadly, East's opening bid and West's failure to raise (holding ♠J–10–x) surely put East with the ♦A. You can avoid a club loser if someone has a ♣Q–x and at most two trumps: draw two rounds of trumps and ruff the fourth club in dummy. Another chance can be to find East with ♣Q–x–x and force him to lead a diamond.

The key plays
1. Cash a top trump from each hand and the ♣A–K.
2. Leaving the last trump out, play a third round of clubs.
3. East wins and, because he has no more trumps, he is stuck.
4. If he plays a spade, you ruff in dummy and discard a diamond from your hand, later getting back to your hand by ruffing (high if need be).
5. If he leads a diamond, dummy's king must score.

IMPORTANT POINT *On this deal you had to leave a trump out to stop East from exiting safely in spades. You would only draw the last trump if you were trying to put West in (with the ♦K in your hand).*

Exiting in the tenace suit

East–West vulnerable
Dealer North

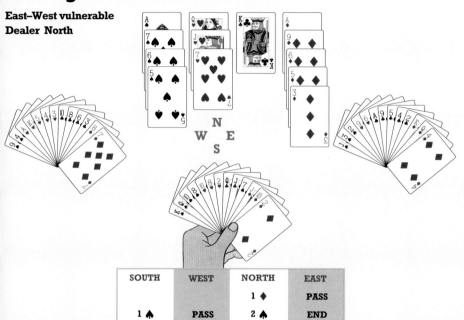

SOUTH	WEST	NORTH	EAST
		1 ♦	PASS
1 ♠	PASS	2 ♠	END

West leads the ace, king, and a third heart. East follows twice and ruffs the third round. He then cashes the ♣A and exits with a club. What is the safest plan for this contract?

What you know
You have lost four tricks and it would take a most unfortunate layout of the trump suit to have a loser there. The main problem is to avoid losing two diamonds if East has the king and queen. What you need to do is to take the first diamond finesse at a time when, if it loses, East can only return a diamond or give a ruff and discard.

The key plays
1. Win the second club in your hand, discarding a diamond from dummy.
2. Cash the ♠A and draw trumps ending in your hand.
3. Cash your other club winner and then run the ♦J.
4. If East returns a diamond, you have a free finesse. If not, discard a diamond from one hand and ruff in the other.
5. If West were able to cover the ♦J, you would win in dummy and easily hold your diamond losers to one.

IMPORTANT POINT *Other sure holdings for a throw in (facing low cards) where you* *cover the second player's card include A–Q–9, K–10–x, K–J–x and Q–J–x.*

Stripping the hand

Both sides vulnerable
Dealer East

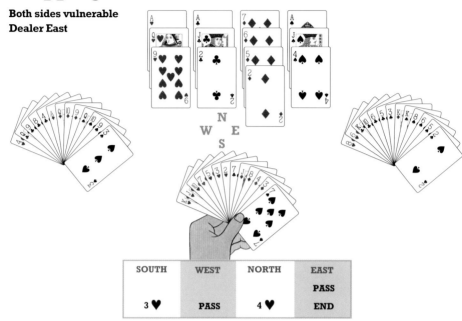

SOUTH	WEST	NORTH	EAST
			PASS
3 ♥	PASS	4 ♥	END

West leads the ♠10. How do you plan the play?

What you know
If West holds four diamonds, you have four losers. Moreover, she would surely have led the suit if she held A–K–Q, and East cannot hold A–K–Q given the lead and his initial pass. So, the diamonds will be blocked if they are four–one. To take advantage of this, you need to make East give you a ruff and discard when in with his top diamond. As entries are scarce, you must start the strip straight away.

The key plays
1. Win the spade and immediately ruff a spade.
2. Go to dummy with a trump, noting that all follow, and ruff again.
3. Cross to the ♣A and ruff a club.
4. Go back to dummy with a trump and ruff another club.
5. Lead a diamond, knowing that the defenders can take at most three tricks before you get a diamond winner or a ruff and discard.

IMPORTANT POINT *Ducking the first round having stripped the hand is also a good way to overcome a four–one break if you have A–8–x–x facing K–7–x–x, K–x–x–x facing Q–x–x–x or A–x–x–x facing J–x–x–x in a side suit.*

Avoidance while stripping

Neither side vulnerable
Dealer South

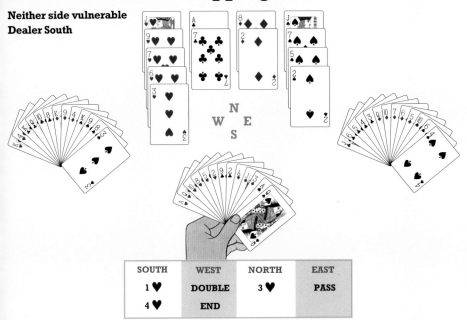

SOUTH	WEST	NORTH	EAST
1 ♥	DOUBLE	3 ♥	PASS
4 ♥	END		

West leads the ♣K. What is the surest line for this contract?

What you know
There is a possible loser in each suit. Although those in the minors look inevitable, a winning spade finesse or successful view in trumps would save you one. Normally you play for the drop with 11 trumps missing the king. There is a case here to finesse if you can arrange that West, upon getting in with the king, has no safe exit. To avoid a spade lead through the A–Q, you must keep East out of the play.

The key plays
1. Duck the first trick so that the ♣J cannot be an entry for East.
2. Win the second club and lead a diamond to the jack (or, if East plays a top honor, win with the ace and exit with the jack).
3. Win the diamond return and ruff a diamond in dummy.
4. Lead a trump, preparing to finesse, but win when East shows out.
5. West, on getting in with the ♥K, must lead a spade or give a ruff and discard.

IMPORTANT POINT *If your diamonds had been weaker, say A–10–x, it would still have been worth leading the suit from dummy. Any time East had only one diamond honor you could keep him out of the play.*

Trump techniques: trump coup

East–West vulnerable
Dealer South

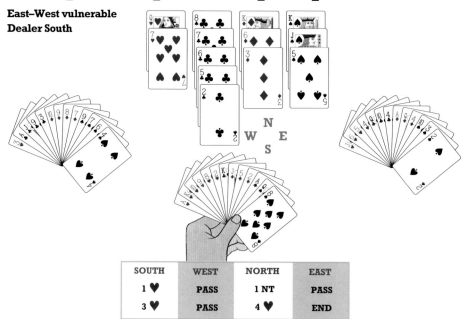

SOUTH	WEST	NORTH	EAST
1 ♥	PASS	1 NT	PASS
3 ♥	PASS	4 ♥	END

West leads the ♦10. East takes the ♦Q and shifts to a club. West wins and returns a club, which you ruff. What is your plan?

What you know

With the ♦A still to lose, all depends on not losing a trump. Since dummy has plenty of entries, you can afford to cash the queen and ace to test the suit. If West shows out, you will have the K–10 over East's J–x but no trump left in dummy to finesse. There is a way around this: have the lead in dummy at trick 12 with the ♥K–10 in your hand. To get there you must reduce your trump length to East's.

The key plays

1. You cash the queen and ace of trumps, finding the four–one break.
2. Lead the ♦J to drive out the ace and win the return in dummy.
3. Ruff a club and cash your remaining side-suit winners to finish with the lead in dummy.
4. You have two clubs left in dummy and the desired ♥K–10 in your hand over East's ♥J–x. You overruff him and so avoid losing a trump.

IMPORTANT POINT *Had the defenders started with three rounds of diamonds, you would have needed to be more precise with* *the timing, leading clubs yourself and ruffing a club when in dummy with the ♥Q.*

Elopement

East–West vulnerable
Dealer South

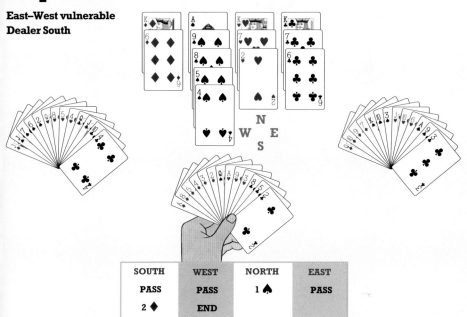

SOUTH	WEST	NORTH	EAST
PASS	PASS	1 ♠	PASS
2 ♦	END		

West leads the ♣Q and, as East has A–x–x, the defenders take the first three tricks. What is your plan when East switches to the ♥J?

What you know

You cannot afford to lose two trumps and a heart as well as the three clubs already lost. If trumps are three–two, there will be no problem, but it is wise to consider a four–one break. To set up and enjoy a long spade you would need four entries to dummy, which you do not have. Even so, ruffing spades is wise. If you can make three small trumps by ruffing, one defender may end up ruffing the other's winning heart.

The key plays

1. To conserve dummy's entry, win the heart in your hand.
2. Play a spade to the ace and ruff a spade—a four–one trump break is far more likely than a six–one spade division.
3. Then, cash the ♦A and ♦K and ruff another spade.
4. Finally, cross to the ♥K and lead a fourth spade. If East ruffs, you throw a loser. If not, you score the vital third ruff.

IMPORTANT POINT *If West was the one with four diamonds, you would need some luck, finding her with a 4–2–4–3 shape.*

When East has four trumps, you can cope with any likely distribution.

Trump endplay

East–West vulnerable
Dealer South

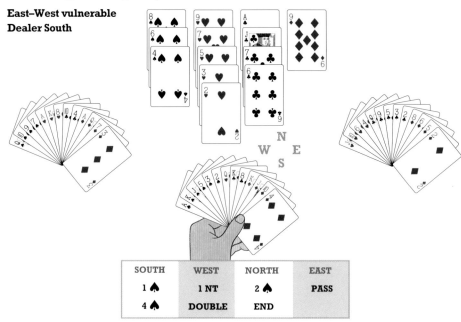

SOUTH	WEST	NORTH	EAST
1 ♠	1 NT	2 ♠	PASS
4 ♠	DOUBLE	END	

West leads top hearts and you ruff the second round. When you play a top spade, East throws a club. What is your plan?

What you know

West, who began with ♠Q–10–9–x has two sure tricks unless you can arrange for her to lead the suit. She will lead a spade of course only if she has nothing else left. If East's club discard is from five, West has a doubleton club. As there are more diamonds than hearts missing, 4–3–4–2 is perhaps her most likely shape. Other things being equal, you plan therefore to ruff one more heart but no clubs.

The key plays

1. Lead a low diamond to set up a ruffing finesse against West's ace.
2. When West takes the queen, win the club return in your hand and play top diamonds, ruffing only when West plays the ace.
3. After that, ruff a heart, cash any diamond winners left, and cross to the ♣A.
4. Finally, duck a trump (or ruff something low) to put West on lead.

IMPORTANT POINT *A trump endplay often involves guesswork. If you thought West was 4–4–3–2, you would ruff two hearts. If you thought she was 4–3–3–3, you would ruff a heart and a club.*

Squeeze techniques: Simple squeeze

North–South vulnerable
Dealer South

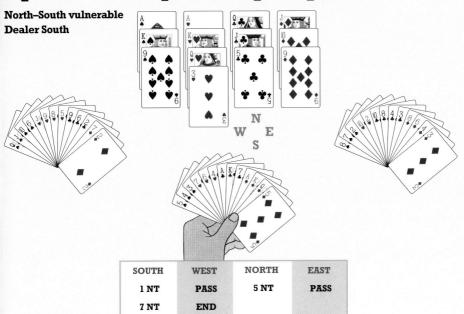

SOUTH	WEST	NORTH	EAST
1 NT	PASS	5 NT	PASS
7 NT	END		

With values all in sequence, you treat your hand as maximum. What is your plan on the ♠Q lead?

What you know

You have twelve top tricks: four diamonds, two spades, and three each in hearts and clubs. The best hope of a thirteenth is a three–three heart break. There is another realistic possibility. If West has Q–J–10–x or any five spades and heart length, you can squeeze her. She discards before dummy, so you can judge what you keep there. To do this successfully, you will need to keep track of what cards she keeps.

The key plays

1. Win the spade and run the diamonds, dummy throwing a club.
2. Cash the other top spade (best) or three top hearts (but not both).
3. Cash the queen followed by the ♣A and ♣K.
4. This last winner squeezes West and, so long as you have kept track of the ♠J–10 (or the missing heart if you cashed three hearts), you will know for sure which of the ♠9 and the ♥3 could be good.

IMPORTANT POINT *The squeeze almost plays itself. You just have to make sure the final minor-suit winner comes from your hand and cash the top cards in one of dummy's threat suits to remove ambiguity.*

Automatic simple squeeze

East–West vulnerable
Dealer South

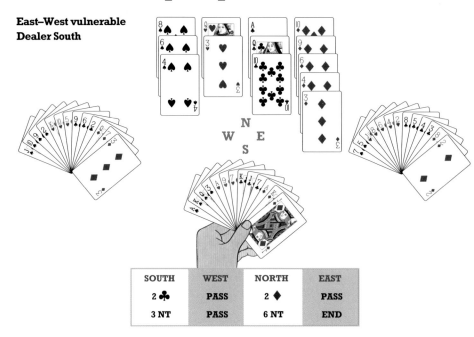

SOUTH	WEST	NORTH	EAST
2 ♣	PASS	2 ♦	PASS
3 NT	PASS	6 NT	END

What is your plan when West leads the ♠J?

What you know
You have nine top tricks. If the diamond suit runs without loss, you will have the three more you need. If not, there is a chance of a three–three spade break or, if one defender holds spade length and the ♥K, of a squeeze. If East has four spades, you can afford to test the spades early because you can keep ♥A–x if he bares his ♥K on the squeeze trick. You need to take more care if West has the spade length.

The key plays
1. Win the spade, cash the ♦A, cross to the ♣10, and lead to the ♦J.
2. When this loses and West leads the ♠10, win and cash the ♦K.
3. You need to keep a spade entry but the ♥A is in the way and you cash this next (a play known as a Vienna coup). Then cash the remaining minor-suit winners.
4. Watch only for the ♥K. If someone discards it, cash the ♥Q. If not, try the spades, hoping they were three–three or that a squeeze has worked.

IMPORTANT POINT *With the count rectified (i.e., all necessary losers lost), you can squeeze either defender if you have a squeeze card and a threat in one hand facing a threat that includes an entry in the other.*

Setting up a squeeze

North–South vulnerable
Dealer East

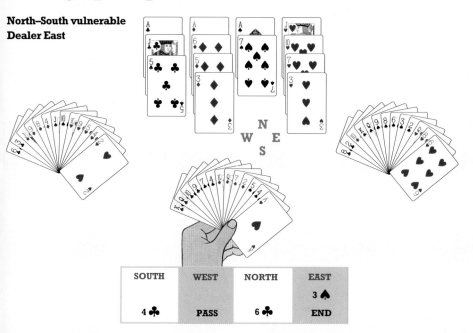

SOUTH	WEST	NORTH	EAST
			3 ♠
4 ♣	PASS	6 ♣	END

West leads the ♠ J. How do you play for this slam?

What you know

You have 11 sure tricks and a three–two diamond break will give you a twelfth. The problem lies in overcoming a four–one break. Even with four diamonds, West may have more hearts than East, suggesting a simple squeeze in the red suits. To prepare for this you need to do two things: make sure that East cannot help guard hearts, and rectify the count by losing the one trick you can afford to lose.

The key plays

1. Win the first spade, cash the ♣K, and unblock the ♥A.
2. Then cross to dummy with a trump, ruff a heart, and lead a spade.
3. Win a diamond return in your hand, cross to dummy with a trump and ruff a second heart.
4. You can cash another top diamond (but not the ace) and finish the trumps. West cannot keep the diamonds guarded and the ♥K.

IMPORTANT POINT *It would also work to discard a spade on a heart rather than giving up a spade. You cannot, however, bring off a throw in to make East give you a ruff and discard because West can win the second spade.*

Double squeeze

Neither side vulnerable
Dealer North

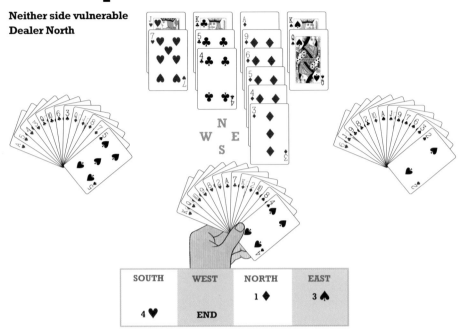

SOUTH	WEST	NORTH	EAST
		1 ♦	3 ♠
4 ♥	END		

West leads the ♠5 to the ace and ruffs the return. She then plays ace and another trump, East showing out. What is your plan?

What you know
You have lost three tricks and cannot afford to lose any more. The obvious parking space for the ♠10 is on a long diamond. You can set that suit up on a three-two break. If West has four diamonds, her shape will be 1–4–4–4 and East's 7–1–1–4. There will be no simple squeeze, as both defenders guard clubs. However, a double squeeze should work

because both defenders are trying to keep clubs and one other suit.

The key plays
1. Win the second heart in your hand and draw the missing trump.
2. Cash the ♦K and ♦A, noting that East shows out.
3. Ruff a diamond (or cross to the club ace) and finish the trumps.
4. On the last trump, West must keep a diamond winner and so unguards clubs. Dummy then throws its last diamond and East, now the only defender guarding clubs, is squeezed in the black suits.

IMPORTANT POINT *For a double squeeze you need winners for all but one of the remaining tricks, a single threat against each* *opponent and a double threat with an entry in its own suit.*

Strip squeeze

Both sides vulnerable
Dealer East

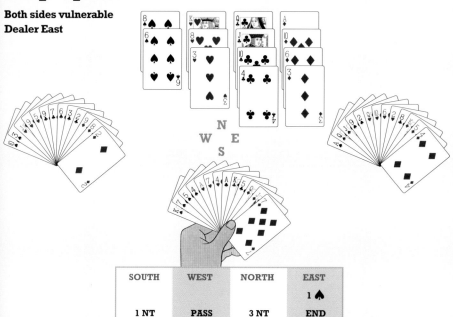

SOUTH	WEST	NORTH	EAST
			1 ♠
1 NT	PASS	3 NT	END

West leads the ♠10, which holds. A second spade goes to East's nine. How do you play?

What you know

You have eight top tricks and the diamond suit offers room for at least two more. The danger is losing four spades and the ♦K. There is no point in holding up again because the diamond finesse goes into East. As you have a tenace in diamonds and are only one trick short, you think of an endplay on East. If he has a doubleton heart, this is easy. If he has more than two, you need to squeeze him.

The key plays

1. Win the second spade to retain a sure exit card.
2. Cash four rounds of clubs, discarding a heart from your hand.
3. If East has thrown a spade, come to your hand and run the ♦Q.
4. If not, he has only four red cards left, presumably including ♦K–x. If so, cash the ♥K and ♥A before exiting with a spade.
5. If you think that East has unguarded the ♦K, cash the ♦A.

IMPORTANT POINT *To execute a strip squeeze you usually need to guess what cards an opponent has kept. Most defenders take* *the path of least resistance, keeping their honors guarded.*

Strip squeeze or simple endplay

East–West vulnerable
Dealer West

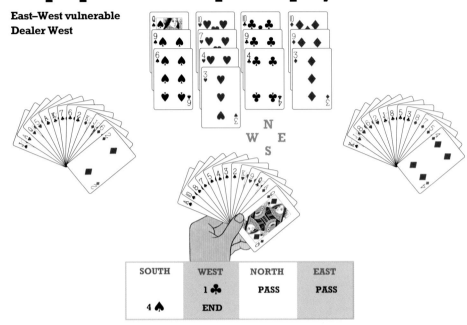

SOUTH	WEST	NORTH	EAST
	1 ♣	PASS	PASS
4 ♠	END		

West cashes the ♣A and continues with the king. You ruff and lay down the ♠A, dropping East's king. How do you play from here?

What you know
East passed West's opening bid and has shown up with the ♠K. This makes it almost certain that West has the ♦K and the ♥A. One option is to cross to dummy with a trump, ruff a club, and exit with the ace and another diamond. If West has a doubleton ♦K, she will be endplayed. This is unlikely and it is a better bet to try to squeeze her down to two diamonds.

The key plays
1. Cross to dummy with the queen of trumps and ruff a club.
2. Then, run the rest of the trumps, reducing everyone to four cards.
3. If you think that West has kept only one diamond, cash the ace.
4. If you think that West has kept only one heart, duck a heart.
5. If, as most players will, West keeps two cards in each red suit, play the ace followed by another diamond to score the ♥K at the end.

IMPORTANT POINT *The strip squeeze usually occurs in a no-trump contract, when there are no trumps left in dummy after drawing trumps or when (as here) you want to exit in an unevenly divided suit (compare with page 197).*

Non-material squeeze

North–South vulnerable
Dealer West

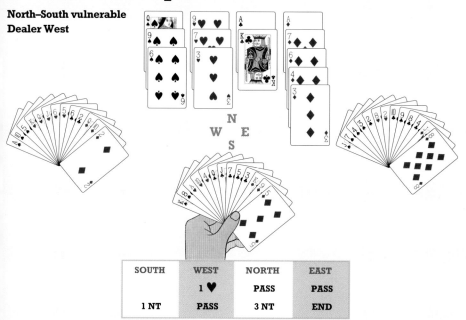

SOUTH	WEST	NORTH	EAST
	1 ♥	PASS	PASS
1 NT	PASS	3 NT	END

West leads the ♥K and, if you hold up, she will continue playing the suit from a holding of K–Q–J–x–x. What is your plan?

What you know
Assuming clubs break no worse than four–two you have eight top tricks. By knocking out the spade ace, you could set up a ninth. The snag is that the bidding virtually marks West with this card, so you would lose four hearts and a spade. West is unlikely to discard a heart if she can help it, but perhaps she will have no choice. If she has three or more diamonds, she could be in trouble protecting three suits.

The key plays
1. Win the third heart to be absolutely sure of the heart layout.
2. Cash the ♣A–K, noting that all follow.
3. Return to the ♦K and finish the clubs.
4. If West discards a heart, you can set up a spade trick.
5. If she discards the ♠A, you make an overtrick.
6. If not, she can have only two diamonds left, so try that suit.

IMPORTANT POINT *For a non-material squeeze, you need to be only one trick short and have threats against a defender in two* *suits apart from the one in which she has winners to cash.*

DEFENDER'S FOLLOWING SUIT

Third hand high

When West leads the three, you should play the ace, not the jack. It is irrelevant that your jack suffices to beat dummy's ten. Declarer probably has a spade higher than the ten. If that card is the king, it makes no difference what you do. When, as here, it is the queen, you can prevent it from winning a trick.

Layout **1**

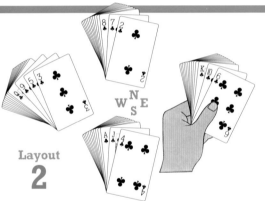

Layout **2**

Again West leads the three and again you play high in third seat, putting up the king. In a suit contract, you do not expect your king to win (because partner will rarely underlead an ace) but you can knock out declarer's ace. As the cards lie, putting in the ten would allow your opponent an undeserved second trick with the jack.

Playing high in third seat has most to gain when declarer holds a singleton honor. On the lead of the jack, East must put up the ace to stop the king from scoring. If West has led from K–J–10, nothing is lost because the suit is still solid for the defenders.

Layout **3**

IMPORTANT POINT
It can be right to play high even when your card is merely equal with partner's. For example, with A–x and the king led or K–x and the queen led, overtaking (if safe to do so) can avoid a blockage.

Finessing against dummy

When dummy has a useful holding, you do not automatically play your highest card in third seat. Here, if you held the ace and queen, it would be clear to play the queen rather than ace if dummy plays low on West's three. As you can see from the layout shown, it is just as important to finesse when partner has the queen and you A–J.

You need not have the ace to finesse. When West and dummy both play low, you must finesse the ten, saving the king to capture the queen. In a suit contract, you can be confident that West has led from the jack rather than the ace. If West does have the ace (in a no-trump contract), then declarer would have a stopper anyway with J–x–x.

Layout
2

Your holding is weaker but so is the honor in dummy against which you finesse (the ten). If, after the two and six are played, you put up the jack, you expect declarer to win and later make the ace and ten by finessing. You cannot do anything about K–9–x on your left, but playing the eight helps if West has Q–9–x–(x) or K–9–x–(x).

Layout
3

IMPORTANT POINT

The usual rule is to finesse against an honor ranking only one or two cards below yours. You do not normally finesse against the ten when holding the king or the jack when holding the ace.

Ducking to maintain communications

When West leads the nine, whether dummy plays high or low, you normally duck, playing the ten to encourage. In a no-trump contract, withholding the ace leaves partner a spade to lead later in the play to help set up your suit. In a suit contract, if you keep communications open by ducking, you may be able to give partner a ruff.

Layout 1

Layout 2

The right play when West leads the ♥7 may depend on the entry position. If you expect to gain the lead first, finesse the jack (or cover the queen) so you can continue the suit. If, in a no-trump contract, you expect partner to get in first, you duck. This stops declarer from holding up and means partner will have a heart left to lead later.

If you need only one club trick, you should play the queen on the first round to force out the ace. When, however, you need either to set up three club tricks or ensure that declarer cannot make three club tricks, you need to duck. The sacrifice comes back with interest when you flush out the ace with a low card on the second round.

Layout 3

IMPORTANT POINT

You duck simply to save a high card if partner has led from rubbish and you have no intermediate cards. For example, if you have K–7–5–4–2, you duck, hoping that declarer has a doubleton or singleton ace.

Touching cards

With two cards of equal rank, in third seat you play the lower one. If you had no agreement and played the queen, partner would hesitate to lead the suit again for fear of setting up declarer's hypothetical jack. Playing the jack is much clearer because South's failure to win cheaply with the queen marks you with this card.

The rule is the same when you finesse. By playing the ten, it is clear who holds the jack when the ten drives out the ace. South would take the ten with the jack if able to do so. By suggesting your holding through playing the ten you encourage partner to continue the suit, which enables you to pick up dummy's queen.

When you are not attempting to win the trick, the rules change. Now, if you have a strong enough sequence to drop a high card, you play the highest card from your sequence. By playing the jack, you warn partner that declarer has the queen and suggest that it might be worth trying to get you on lead to play the second round of hearts.

IMPORTANT POINT
The times to play the higher of touching cards to a trick not yet won are rare: when you want to encourage partner to switch despite your strength or when you want to deceive declarer about your holding.

Attitude signals on partner's lead

When partner leads and you are not trying to win the trick, you usually signal to say whether you want the suit led again. With the queen led and the ace played, you play your lowest card, the two, to discourage. This warns partner that you cannot offer any help in the suit and that continuing it may be either pointless or risky or both.

Layout
2

Again West leads the queen and dummy plays the ace. This time, you hold the king and should be happy to have the suit continued. To encourage you play the highest card that you can afford, the eight. You would also encourage, at least in a no-trump contract, if you held 10–8–x. Your ten would make it safe for partner to continue hearts.

In a suit contract, you might encourage because you are short in the suit rather than because you have strength in it. If partner leads the ace (or whatever you lead from A–K and others), you can picture a ruff on the third round. Assuming you can ruff, you play the ten to ask partner to continue the suit. The ten could also be from Q–10–x.

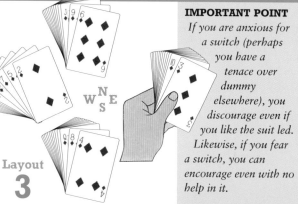

Layout
3

IMPORTANT POINT
If you are anxious for a switch (perhaps you have a tenace over dummy elsewhere), you discourage even if you like the suit led. Likewise, if you fear a switch, you can encourage even with no help in it.

Count signals on partner's lead

If your like or dislike of the suit led is clear, even without a signal, you show count rather than attitude. When West leads a top spade and sees dummy, she knows you have only low cards but not (in a suit contract) whether declarer might ruff the next round. With three cards, an odd number, you play the five, your lowest card.

When partner leads the king, you know declarer will win with the ace (either because it is a singleton or to set up dummy's jack). Partner will again know you have only low cards but not how many. In a count situation, you play high with an even number—your higher card with a doubleton or second highest from four.

When her queen holds, partner will put you with the ace and jack. Therefore, you can show your length in the suit. With an even number you play high, the jack. If you had five hearts or seven, you would play low instead. Partner can often tell from the bidding (declarer's or yours), exactly how many cards an odd or even number means.

IMPORTANT POINT
Some people play that certain leads ask for a count signal or for partner to either unblock (with an honor) or show count. In this case, assuming it is safe to do so, you give the type of signal requested.

Second hand low

Playing low in second seat is the norm when declarer attacks a suit by leading low. Whatever high cards you have you want to save for the second or later rounds so that you can capture something with them. If you played the ace on the six, you would allow declarer three tricks. It is better to save the ace to stop the queen from scoring.

Layout **1**

Holding the king, it is still right to play low here. If you rose with the king on the two, either the queen or jack would drive out the ace and declarer would have a third-round winner. By playing low, you allow partner to capture the jack with the ace. This leaves you with the K–10 as a tenace over the queen.

Layout **2**

If you can do so without hesitation, you should play low on this layout as well. If your objective is two tricks and you think declarer has a doubleton, you must play low in the hope that partner has the queen and that your opponent misguesses. Going in with the ace would be correct only if one trick is all you need.

Layout **3**

IMPORTANT POINT
When dummy comes down you should study the holdings there that declarer might lead toward. This means that, when the time comes, you should be able to play low smoothly when it is right to do so.

Winning quickly

East–West vulnerable
Dealer South

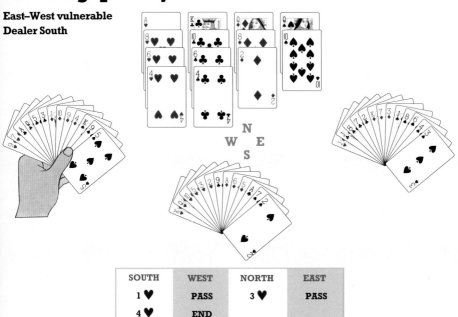

SOUTH	WEST	NORTH	EAST
1 ♥	PASS	3 ♥	PASS
4 ♥	END		

You lead the ♦J to the two, seven, and ace. Declarer cashes the ♥A and ♥K, on which East plays the ♥J and the ♠3, and leads the ♣9.

What you know

The ♦7 at trick one looks encouraging and perhaps you can make two diamond tricks. These plus one in each black suit would defeat the contract. Since you have the A–Q in clubs, you know that declarer cannot make a losing guess. In spades there could be a guess in some situations with the queen and ten in dummy, but here you need only one spade trick.

The key plays

1. Take the ♣A at once—South might (and does) have a singleton.
2. Continue with the ♦9 (partner already knows you have the ♦10).
3. When dummy covers and partner plays a third round, you win.
4. To avoid giving a ruff and discard (which the ♦4 would) or allowing declarer to take a winning guess in spades, exit with a club.
5. Later, if declarer leads a low spade from his hand, take the king.

IMPORTANT POINT *The times to grab an honor quickly are when an opponent is short in the suit or when you know declarer cannot* *have a guess, or when you are taking the setting trick.*

Splitting honors

If declarer leads a low spade from dummy then you should play the jack or queen. This way you ensure one trick in the suit. If you played low, declarer might put in the ten and now have no loser. Opinions vary on the right specific card. In a suit that an opponent chooses to play, it is probably best to play at random.

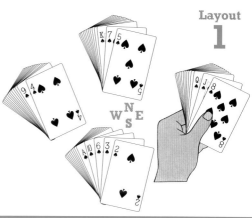

Layout

1

The right play depends on your objective in the suit. If you need to hold declarer to one trick, you should play low on the four in the hope that partner has the ten and that declarer finesses the nine from dummy. If, instead, you just need one club trick, you should play high so that the jack (or nine) cannot be a cheap first-round winner.

Layout

2

Imagine that dummy leads this suit late in the play, when you know that partner has no safe exit cards outside hearts. If you play the four, declarer can take a deep finesse of the eight to put West on play. To stop this from happening you must split your honors. Indeed, even with only J–x–x or 10–x–x it would be right to play high.

Layout

3

IMPORTANT NOTE
Splitting your honors is wrong if your length tells you that declarer does not plan to finesse immediately. For example, with four low trumps in dummy and J–10–9–x in your hand, play low in case partner is void.

Covering honors

When the queen is led, you must cover with the king. By doing so you promote partner's ten to winning rank on the third round. Yes, if South has the ten, covering does not help but, in that situation, your side can never make a heart trick. The important point is that your king is dead anyway but covering may help partner's holding.

Layout
1

Layout
2

With the jack led from dummy you should cover with the queen. This saves a trick if partner has either K–9–x or A–9–x because the nine will become significant. If you mistakenly allowed the jack to run, partner would win it. Then declarer would just need an entry to dummy to repeat the finesse and pick up the suit for one loser.

With length in the suit but poor intermediates, covering ceases to be wise. If you cover the queen with the king, you will find that you have promoted nothing. The point here is that declarer can finesse only twice and (barring a trump coup) your king cannot be caught.

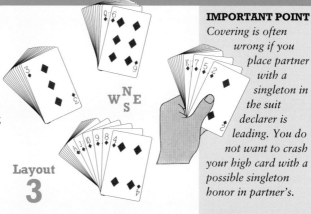

Layout
3

IMPORTANT POINT
Covering is often wrong if you place partner with a singleton in the suit declarer is leading. You do not want to crash your high card with a possible singleton honor in partner's.

Covering touching cards

Covering the queen on the first round would be wrong. Declarer wins with the ace and runs the nine on the way back; your side fails to take a spade trick. It is much better to let the queen hold and wait to cover the jack. This way partner's ten wins on the third round. It is usually right to cover the last of touching honors.

Layout **1**

Layout **2**

You should not cover the jack for two reasons. The first is that declarer might hold K–x, when covering could resolve a guess in the suit. The second is that your opponent could hold A–x–x. If you play the queen at once, dummy's ten will become good. Correct is to let partner win the first club to leave you with Q–9 over dummy's 10–x.

When you have two honors higher than the one led, you should cover. Is it better to play the ace or the queen on the jack? See what happens if you play the ace: later you cover the ten with the queen to set up West's nine. Covering with the queen does not work so well as declarer wins with the king and runs the eight on the way back.

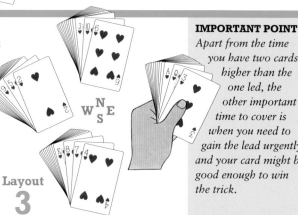

Layout **3**

IMPORTANT POINT

Apart from the time you have two cards higher than the one led, the other important time to cover is when you need to gain the lead urgently and your card might be good enough to win the trick.

Count signals on declarer's lead

When declarer leads the king and partner ducks, you should play the two. In a suit led by the opposition, a low card suggests an odd number of cards in the suit (here, three). This will help partner decide whether to take the ace on the second round. It is likely to be right to do so even if dummy does have a side entry.

Layout
1

W N E S

Layout
2

To show an even number you begin a high–low. If you can afford it, play high from a doubleton and, with four cards, play your second-highest. By playing the nine under the ace you imply a four-card holding, so partner can figure out the suit is not running. Note that partner does not drop the ten—South might hold A–9 doubleton.

Beware of giving away the position if you think that a count signal will help declarer more than partner. If declarer cashes three top hearts and then abandons the suit, partner can guess that you have the fourth round covered. To announce earlier that you have four cards might lead declarer to finesse successfully against your jack.

Layout
3

IMPORTANT POINT
Some duplicate players use reverse signals, low from even and high from odd. Some also use reverse attitude, low to encourage. The methods have a slight technical advantage but are not that popular.

Trump echo

Both sides vulnerable
Dealer North

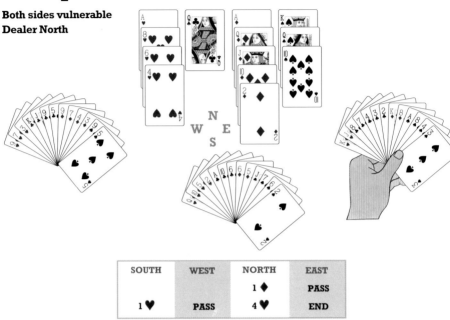

SOUTH	WEST	NORTH	EAST
		1 ♦	PASS
1 ♥	PASS	4 ♥	END

West leads the ♠9. You win and return a spade, all following. The ♥A and the ♥4 come next, on which West plays the ♥7 and ♥3.

What you know
You have two tricks—a spade and a heart—and hope to score a diamond as well. The fourth trick could be a spade ruff, if partner has a trump left, or the club ace. What does partner's high–low in trumps mean? Traditionally it shows a third trump with which to ruff. If, instead, you play suit-preference signals (a treatment some duplicate players use), the seven on the first round must deny club values.

The key plays
1. Lead a third round of spades. Partner's high low in spades as well as in trumps tells you a ruff is likely.
2. Sooner or later, declarer must take the diamond finesse and your king will take the setting trick.
3. If partner played upward in spades (not possible on this occasion after the lead of the nine) or in trumps, you would try a club instead.

IMPORTANT POINT *Do not routinely signal trump length because declarer often wants to know how the suit is breaking. Do so when* *partner needs to know, for instance, if there is a chance of a forcing game or to count declarer's tricks.*

Capturing honors

You need to capture the jack with the ace if declarer leads or leads up to the jack. Likewise, partner needs to capture the queen with the king or the nine with the ten if declarer leads up to one of those cards. Winning a trick is a natural thing to do, even more so when you can capture an opposing high card in doing so.

Layout
1

Layout
2

If declarer finesses the queen, you should take the king. When you cannot see the jack, there is a chance that partner has it. Whenever this is the case, ducking would allow declarer an undeserved second heart trick.

Winning is so natural that it is wise to know the exceptions. Suppose a lead goes to dummy's king and you take the ace. On the second round declarer will surely finesse the ten. It is a different story if you duck smoothly. Might your opponent not then play to the queen on the second round, placing West with the ace?

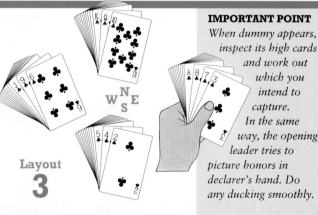

Layout
3

IMPORTANT POINT

When dummy appears, inspect its high cards and work out which you intend to capture. In the same way, the opening leader tries to picture honors in declarer's hand. Do any ducking smoothly.

Holding up

East–West vulnerable
Dealer North

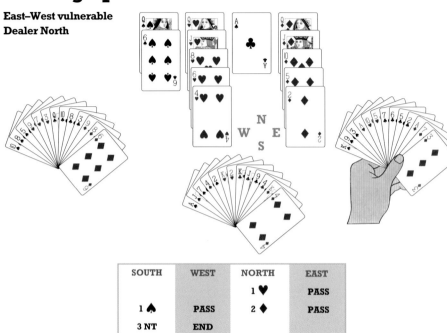

SOUTH	WEST	NORTH	EAST
		1 ♥	PASS
1 ♠	PASS	2 ♦	PASS
3 NT	END		

Dummy wins West's ♣3 lead and leads the ♦2. What do you do?

What you know

The opponents seem to have game values and a source of tricks in at least two suits (the red suits). Moreover, your flat shape and ♠K suggest that the cards are lying well for the other side. Perhaps you can find a way to give declarer communication problems, making it impossible to get to dummy. You want to take each of your red aces on declarer's last card in the respective suits.

The key plays

1. You should duck the first diamond, noting that West plays the six.
2. Seeing her play upward on the next round to signify a three-card holding (her odd number cannot be five), you win the second round of diamonds.
3. You return a club, which West wins cheaply before trying a spade.
4. You finesse the ♠9 (or cover the queen) and hold up in hearts in the same way, winning the second round, before going back to clubs.

IMPORTANT POINT *When you returned a club you should have played the five. You were unable to return your original fourth* *highest because you played the two at trick one to discourage clubs.*

Suit preference signals

You play the two under partner's ace to show an odd number. On the second round, having already given your primary signal, you express suit preference. Play your lower remaining card to imply interest in the lower-ranking (non-trump) suit and your higher card to imply interest in the higher-ranking suit.

Layout **1**

Layout **2**

On the first round you play the seven, second-highest being normal with four cards in the suit. This time you have a three-way choice on the next round. The nine shows interest in a high-ranking suit and the three interest in a low-ranking suit. The six, the normal follow-up card, implies no preference between those two suits.

If dummy has plenty of trumps (making a switch attractive), give a suit-preference signal on partner's king lead. If spades are trumps, the jack asks for a diamond and the three for a club. With little preference between the minors, you would play a middling card. You could also overtake—surely right if you want hearts continued.

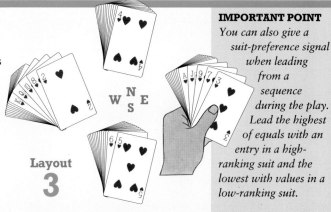

Layout **3**

IMPORTANT POINT
You can also give a suit-preference signal when leading from a sequence during the play. Lead the highest of equals with an entry in a high-ranking suit and the lowest with values in a low-ranking suit.

DEFENSIVE LEADS AND SWITCHES

Choice of card on return

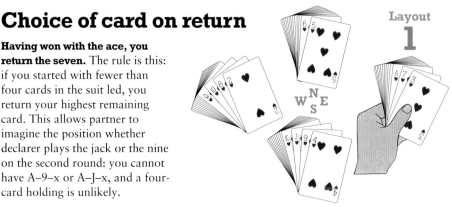

Layout 1

Having won with the ace, you return the seven. The rule is this: if you started with fewer than four cards in the suit led, you return your highest remaining card. This allows partner to imagine the position whether declarer plays the jack or the nine on the second round: you cannot have A–9–x or A–J–x, and a four-card holding is unlikely.

Layout 2

With four (or more cards) in the suit led, return your original fourth highest. After a heart to the ace and the three back to the ten and jack, partner should know the position. In a no-trump contract it will be almost certain that the hearts are running; in a suit contract it will be clear that playing a third heart will not give a ruff and discard.

The right return depends on your objective. If you need to cash the first five tricks (in a no-trump contract), you return the ten, your "normal" higher card. This avoids blocking the suit if the lead comes from K–9–x–x–x. However, in a suit contract, or if you think partner has an outside entry, you can save your ten and return the safe seven.

Layout 3

IMPORTANT POINT

Returning partner's suit is often a good idea. Partner must have had some reason for leading the suit in the first place. In addition, when you open up a new suit, you risk losing a trick about 40% of the time.

Plugging away at a weak spot

East–West vulnerable
Dealer South

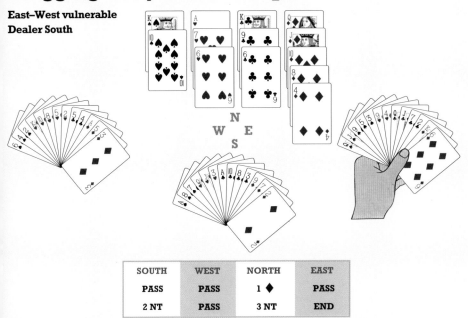

SOUTH	WEST	NORTH	EAST
PASS	PASS	1 ♦	PASS
2 NT	PASS	3 NT	END

West leads the ♥5 and your nine loses to the queen. Declarer runs the ♦9. What are your plans?

What you know

Assuming the lead is fourth highest, West must have three hearts higher than the five. You can see four between your hand and dummy, so South has two, including the queen already played. You can deduce that declarer's other high heart is not the king, for West would lead the jack from J–10–8–x–x. You can also place West with the ♦A—otherwise declarer would have crossed to dummy and finessed.

The key plays

1. You should win the diamond with the king. This saves a trick if West holds A–x and lets you play hearts from your side of the table.

2. You should return a heart. This way, when West gets in with a diamond, the suit will be ready to run. Indeed, as a rule, you should return the suit partner leads unless you see good reason not to.

IMPORTANT POINT *If West had led a spade (perhaps because you had made a light overcall), continuing the suit led would again* *be a good idea. This time West would win the first diamond to conserve your entry.*

Making declarer ruff

Neither side vulnerable
Dealer South

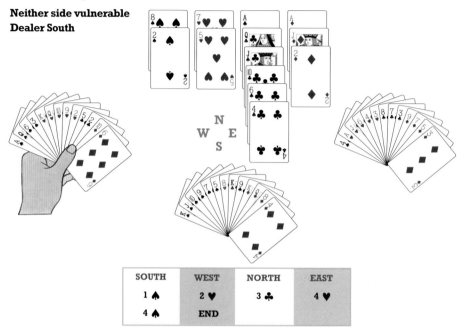

SOUTH	WEST	NORTH	EAST
1 ♠	2 ♥	3 ♣	4 ♥
4 ♠	END		

You lead the ♥K and, when partner plays the three (count signals apply when attitude is obvious) and it holds, you continue the suit. Declarer ruffs the second round, crosses to the ♦A, and runs the ♠8.

What you know
Given South's bidding, partner can hardly hold a king as well as the ♥A. You therefore need three trump tricks to defeat the contract. To achieve this you must make South ruff twice more so that you will end up with the long trump. Since dummy is out of hearts, it is no good winning the first spade and playing a heart.

The key plays
1. You should duck the first spade and win the second cheaply.
2. Then continue with a third round of hearts, forcing South to ruff.
3. If declarer tries another trump, win at once and play a fourth heart to put the contract two down. (You will make a long heart later.)
4. If declarer abandons trumps, you will score a ruff to put the contract one down.

IMPORTANT POINT *Note the technique of plugging away your long suit, just as you would in a no-trump contract. Note also the* *hold-up in trumps so that dummy could not take one of the heart forces.*

Danger of opening up a new suit

The more the honors are spread around the table the riskier it is to open up the suit. As East you want to save your king to capture the queen. A spade switch will not do you much good unless partner has A–J–10 or, if you just need two tricks, she has the ace. A spade lead from West is also costly whenever declarer has A–10–x or K–10–x.

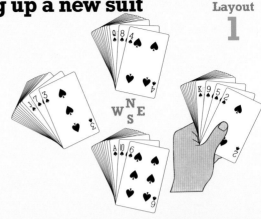

South's ♣9 makes it costly for West to lead a club. By playing low from dummy on the three, declarer picks up the queen. For a club switch to work, East would either need the king or the queen and nine. As the cards lie, a club switch from East also costs and would only bear fruit if you had K–10–9.

If you lead a low heart, declarer may guess to play dummy's ten and so avoid a loser in the suit. Normally you would only lead a heart if dummy has a source of tricks in another suit and you would not score a heart by defending passively. If East were to lead a heart, declarer would clearly have no first- or second-round heart loser.

IMPORTANT POINT
The riskiest lead is round to an honor that ranks just below yours (for example, you have the king over dummy's queen). Even a lead from low cards is risky if declarer may have a two-way finesse in the suit.

Attacking an entry

North–South vulnerable
Dealer South

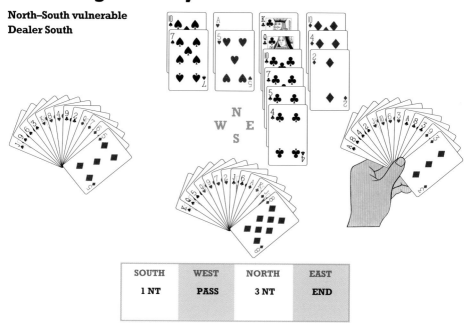

SOUTH	WEST	NORTH	EAST
1 NT	PASS	3 NT	END

After this strong no-trump sequence, West leads the ♠3. As East, what are your plans here?

What you know
Since you can see the ♠2, you know the lead is almost certainly from a four-card suit. If partner has king–queen or king–jack of spades, you can beat the contract with a spade return. If not, you surely need to prevent declarer from enjoying the clubs. You can hold up your ♣A, until the third round if need be, but there is that ♥A sitting in dummy. You need to dislodge that entry first—spades can wait.

The key plays
1. Having won the spade, switch to a heart—low is best because South, with Q–9–x of hearts, would play the queen whatever you do.
2. West covers South's card and, if need be, continues the suit.
3. When a low club comes off dummy you duck.
4. Then, when West follows to the second club, you know declarer has no more. You therefore win and go back to spades.

IMPORTANT POINT *If your hearts were K–10–6–3 (and partner had J–8–4), you would still need to return a heart. Moreover, to make sure of knocking out the ace, you would need to lead the king!*

Drawing dummy's trumps

Both sides vulnerable
Dealer South

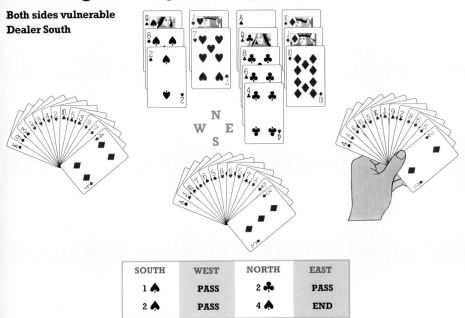

SOUTH	WEST	NORTH	EAST
1 ♠	PASS	2 ♣	PASS
2 ♠	PASS	4 ♠	END

West leads the ♥2 and your king wins. As East, what is your plan to defeat this contract?

What you know

To lead the ♥2, West must have only four hearts (three is unlikely). Since a fourth-highest lead indicates some strength, and you can see the ace, king, jack, and ten, her hearts must include the queen. This means declarer started with three low hearts and, with the doubleton visible in dummy, you should see the threat of a ruff.

The key plays

1. You should switch to a trump and declarer will probably duck, losing to the king.
2. West will play a second round of trumps, on which you discard a diamond; your opponent will most likely win this in dummy and try the ♥J.
3. Since you have no trumps left, you duck this second round of hearts. You might do so even if you were unsure who had the queen. This allows partner to win and play a third round of trumps.

IMPORTANT POINT *On this deal, an additional factor was that you had the clubs well covered. In general, a trump switch is more dangerous if you think that dummy's long suit will be easy to set up.*

Leading up to weakness

Leading up to a weak suit in dummy is often a good idea, setting up or cashing tricks for your side in safety. Usually you lead the same card as on the opening lead, such as fourth highest or top of a sequence. In a no-trump contract, if you lead the three, West can win cheaply, put you back in with the ace, and win two more tricks.

A switch to the ♥J is attractive here. If partner has the ace and queen, you might cash three tricks at once. It also works well on the layout shown. If declarer ducks or covers with the queen, your side can safely continue the suit. Best is to grab the ace. Even then, if you regain the lead, a second heart lead gives your side two tricks.

Layout
2

Normally you would shift to a low card. Then, if West has A–10–x or Q–x–x, it will be safe for her to continue the suit. When, however, you need to cash out, scoring three quick tricks (four in a no-trump contract) lead the jack. Leading low from this holding (or Q–x–x) will not work because declarer will duck and leave partner on lead.

Layout
3

IMPORTANT POINT
After the first trick you lead the king from A–K. Partner then gives a count signal on the king and an attitude signal on the ace.

Leading an unusual card

Both sides vulnerable
Dealer North

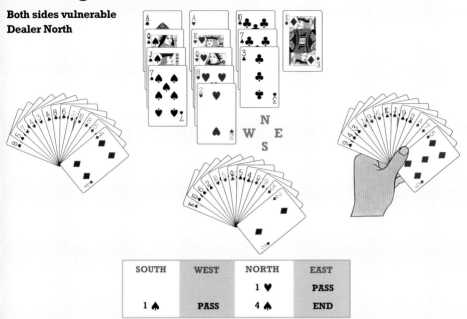

SOUTH	WEST	NORTH	EAST
		1 ♥	PASS
1 ♠	PASS	4 ♠	END

West leads the ♦J and your ace wins. What do you return?

What you know
Dummy's holdings in the majors tell you that there are no tricks for your side there, so you need three in clubs. With a specific objective in mind, it is often right to lead a card you would not lead originally. Here, with ♣A–K–x, you would lead low so that declarer, with Q–x–x, would have the losing option of running it around to dummy. On your actual holding you do not want declarer to have that choice.

The key plays
1. You should switch to the ♣J, the card you would lead if you had K–J–10–x or A–J–10–x. Since your jack and nine are the cards above and below the ten, you may hear this called a "surrounding" play. The same play by declarer would be called a backward finesse.
2. If South ducks, your side's A–K of clubs take the next two tricks.
3. If South covers, West wins and you have K–9 over dummy's 10–x.

IMPORTANT POINT *The position is similar if you hold K–10–8–x or Q–10–8–x. If you can see 9–x–x or A–9–x on your right or J–x–x or A–J–x on your left, switch to the ten. This sets up two tricks if partner has Q–x–x or K–x–x.*

Ruff and discard danger

East–West vulnerable
Dealer East

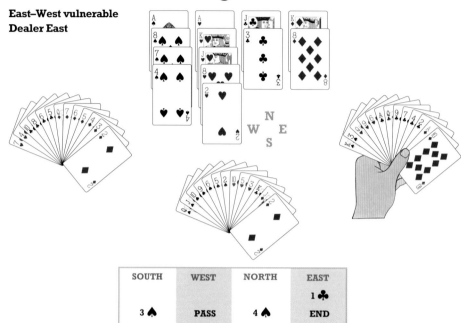

SOUTH	WEST	NORTH	EAST
			1 ♣
3 ♠	PASS	4 ♠	END

West leads the ♣5 and your ace drops the king. Declarer ruffs your ♣Q and plays two rounds of trumps, West throwing two diamonds. What is your plan?

What you know
You have made two tricks and the ♦A will be a third. To defeat the contract it looks like you need to make a second diamond or the ♥Q. A heart return is most unattractive since the entire suit will run. Even if declarer has a singleton heart and needs to ruff one round, that will be enough. A club return is just as bad. Declarer can discard a heart from his hand, ruff in dummy, and set up the hearts with a ruff.

The key plays
1. Counting declarer for eight black cards and so five red cards, you work out that a heart trick cannot run away if you lead a diamond.
2. You do not want to be thrown in again, so lead the ♦A followed by a low diamond.
3. If declarer runs some trumps before taking the heart finesse, you can safely discard clubs. Eventually your ♥Q takes the setting trick.

IMPORTANT POINT *Leading a suit of which both declarer and dummy are void when both have trumps left gives a ruff and discard. Your opponent ruffs in one hand and discards a loser from the other—not usually good for you.*

Safety with a ruff and discard

East–West vulnerable
Dealer South

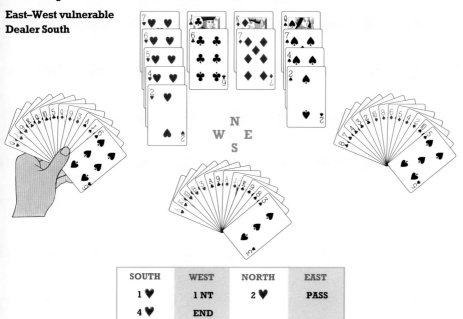

SOUTH	WEST	NORTH	EAST
1 ♥	1 NT	2 ♥	PASS
4 ♥	END		

You lead the ♣K, which loses to the ace. Declarer takes two top trumps, on which East discards diamonds, and the ♦A–K before giving you a club. What is your plan to get off lead?

What you know

You have three sure winners—one spade, one heart, and one club. To beat this contract you need to make a second spade trick. If you lead a spade, you stand little chance because South surely holds the ♠K. Although a lead of either minor may concede a ruff and discard, this will not cost if South is 4–5–2–2.

The key plays

1. You should work out that, holding three cards in one minor, South would have ruffed the third round before putting you on lead.
2. Not wanting to be on lead again, cash your master heart.
3. Then lead a minor (it does not matter which if partner has shown an odd number of clubs and an even number of diamonds). Declarer can discard one spade but must still lose two if East holds 10–x and probably will if East holds 9–x.

IMPORTANT POINT *A ruff and discard is safe when declarer has nothing useful to discard. If your side has cashed its side winners, a ruff and discard can be a potent weapon in a forcing game or for a trump promotion.*

DEFENDER'S DISCARDS AND RUFFS

Throwing losers

Discard means reject as useless, and the norm is to throw useless cards. After partner leads the queen, you can safely discard all your hearts. You would like to keep a low one, though, to keep in touch with partner. In a no-trump contract, West wants to keep her hearts so that the defenders can take four tricks.

Layout
1

Layout
2

If West leads two top hearts and declarer ruffs, neither defender needs to keep any hearts. With declarer and dummy both known to be void, heart discards are safe. Why might you save one? Perhaps declarer wants to get a sure count on the hand or is short of trumps. Alternatively, it may give you a safe exit after dummy is out of trumps.

Even in a no-trump contract, you are unlikely to have time to score your long diamonds, making them safe discards. Indeed, with the king in declarer's hand, you can afford to throw them all away. Now suppose that three rounds have already been played. If you cannot get the lead, again your two long cards are dispensable.

Layout
3

> **IMPORTANT POINT**
> *You can safely discard long cards in a suit if you have no entry to them or they would be ruffed. You can also discard suits that partner can look after or to which declarer has no entry.*

Keeping winners

To stop declarer from setting up a heart you simply need to keep the ace and queen. However, coming down to a doubleton will block the suit, stopping your side from cashing its winners. In a no-trump contract, you want to keep all four of your hearts if you can. In a suit contract it will invariably suffice to keep just A–Q–x.

Layout 1

Again, how many cards to keep depends on the contract. If this is a side suit, you surely just need to keep A–K–J. If declarer cannot afford to lose the lead twice, or if dummy has no entry, keeping A–K is good enough. In a no-trump contract, by contrast, you want to keep all your hearts if partner might gain the lead.

Layout 2

Your long card will normally be dispensable but you want to save three cards if you can. This will keep communications open if partner has A–10–x or K–10–x. You want to try hard to keep at least two cards. Reducing to a bare honor concedes a trick on the second round if South has K–10–x (as shown) and on the third if South has K–x–x.

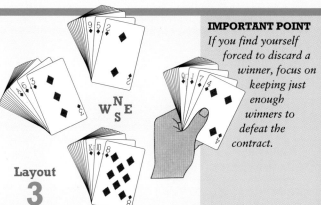

Layout 3

IMPORTANT POINT
If you find yourself forced to discard a winner, focus on keeping just enough winners to defeat the contract.

Keeping potential winners

With the four strong hearts in dummy, as East it is clear to keep your jack guarded. Unless partner also has four hearts (a possibility you might exclude if South has opened 1NT for instance), discarding a heart would set up dummy's four as a winner.

Layout
1

With the length in the closed hand, the position is less clear. If South has K–Q–J–x, West can afford to discard a heart. When, in fact, partner has Q–x or J–x, releasing a heart costs a trick. Often there will be clues from the bidding— suits declarer has bid, or known short suits elsewhere— to tell you where there might be concealed length.

Layout
2

A single discard from a five-card suit is often safe but a second is often risky, especially if you know that an opponent has four cards in the suit. If East throws two diamonds then declarer, in a suit contract, might cash the A–K and ruff the third round. Even in a no-trump contract, declarer could set up a long card by giving up a diamond.

Layout
3

IMPORTANT POINT

Try to keep as many cards as dummy does in its long suit(s) and try also to maintain parity with any length declarer may have. If you cannot do both, guard suits held on your right.

Signals with discards

Playing natural discards, you encourage (ask for) a suit by throwing a high card while a low card discourages. Assuming this is a side suit you can usually spare the nine and this is what you discard. Partner, if he discards a spade, will throw the two; this warns you that declarer holds the king.

Layout 1

The discard of an honor shows the card immediately below it and, by virtue of your ability to spare the card, a strong holding in the suit. In a suit contract, or if three club tricks will suffice to beat a no-trump contract, you discard the ♣J. An honor discard shows either a sequence or, as here, an interior sequence.

Layout 2

If your attitude for a suit is clear, a discard shows your length. With these hearts in dummy partner surely wants to know when to take her ace more than anything else. As with count signals following suit, a low card shows an odd number and a high card an even number. Here you throw the three and West may put South with a singleton.

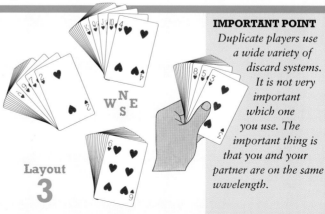

Layout 3

Discarding on partner's winners

Neither side vulnerable
Dealer South

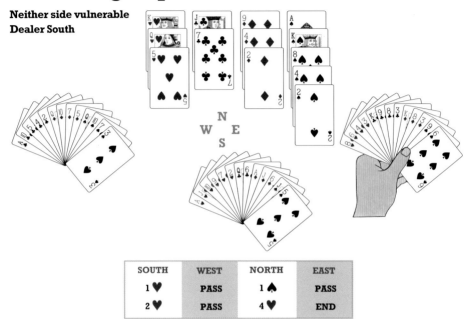

SOUTH	WEST	NORTH	EAST
1 ♥	PASS	1 ♠	PASS
2 ♥	PASS	4 ♥	END

West leads the ♦5 to the king and ace. After a spade to the ace comes the king and a low spade. What are your plans here?

What you know

With a collection of "worthless" trumps, it seems tempting to ruff. The trouble is that you may well be overruffed. In this case, declarer will ruff one more spade to set up the suit and draw trumps ending in dummy. With ♠Q–x–x in his hand, declarer's play would be weird—why block the suit and why play it before drawing trumps? Therefore, you know the spade position even if partner has not given a count signal.

The key plays

1. You should discard the ♦3 (to deny holding the ♦J) or the ♣9 (to encourage clubs). Do not ruff!

2. When declarer ruffs, crosses to dummy with a trump (on which West shows out), and leads another spade, throw a low club.

3. If declarer goes back to dummy and leads the long spade, now you ruff. Later you will come in with the ♣K and return a diamond. This will give your side two tricks in each minor to defeat the contract.

IMPORTANT POINT *Beware of ruffing partner's trick, or one to which declarer need not play a winner. In this case, you would* *normally ruff only if you need to gain the lead quickly or to promote a trump trick for partner.*

Ruffing declarer's winners

Neither side vulnerable
Dealer South

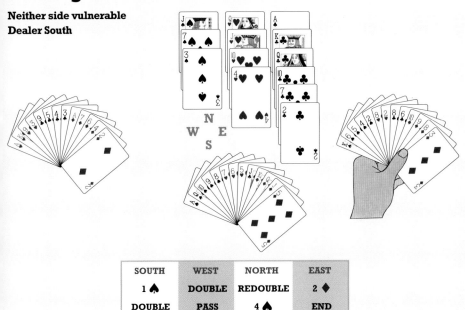

SOUTH	WEST	NORTH	EAST
1 ♠	DOUBLE	REDOUBLE	2 ♦
DOUBLE	PASS	4 ♠	END

North–South play that 2♣ after the double would not be forcing. West leads the ace, king, and a third heart. What are your ruffing plans?

What you know
Partner would hardly have continued with a third heart if you were going to be overruffed. This gives you three tricks: two hearts and a ruff. If partner has the ♦A, you can force dummy to ruff and then your king of trumps will be guarded again. However, you need to take care that declarer does not overruff you at any point.

To avoid that danger you must take care what you ruff later.

The key plays
1. Ruff the third heart and it is best to switch to the ♦10.
2. When dummy ruffs West's ace and leads the ♠J, you duck.
3. If dummy leads a heart next, you discard, a club for preference.
4. If instead, declarer repeats the spade finesse and plays clubs (with or without cashing some diamonds), you discard. Declarer has a trump more than you and will have to ruff before you do.

IMPORTANT POINT *The norm is only to ruff with a natural winner if you need to gain the lead quickly or to disrupt opposing communications. Sacrifice a trump trick only if you expect two tricks in return.*

The uppercut

Declarer, with the lead, could draw trumps (spades). In fact, you have the lead and play a suit that you know your partner and declarer are void in. If partner has J–x, Q–x, K–x, or just a singleton honor and ruffs high, what is declarer to do? Discarding gives your partner a trump trick at once, while overruffing sets up one for you.

Layout **1**

Layout **2**

It is harder work now. Again, you lead a suit of which both unseen hands are void. East ruffs with the ♠7 (the rule is to ruff high, which this is with the ♠8 in dummy) and South overruffs. On the first round of trumps, you capture an honor with the ace. You lead the side suit once more and East's ruff with the nine promotes your ten.

Rarely can you promote a trump trick for yourself by ruffing high. Suppose, however, that the bidding marks you with the queen of the trump suit, hearts (or length in the suit). Given the chance, declarer would then pick up your queen by finessing. If you can ruff with the eight to drive out the ace, this will no longer be possible.

Layout **3**

IMPORTANT POINT
If there is a card in dummy you can cover, uppercut with your next highest card. For example, with a bare trump jack there and Q–9 in your hand, ruffing with the nine gains if partner has 10–x, 8–x–x, or 7–x–x–x.

When not to overruff

Forcing declarer to ruff high
is another good way to
promote a trump trick.
Suppose partner leads a suit
in which you and South are
void. If declarer ruffs with
an honor, it would be wrong
to overruff. The ace is all
you would score. If you
discard instead, your A–10–x
will be worth two tricks
because South has had to
waste an honor.

Layout
1

**The rule is to not overruff
with a natural trump winner.**
If South ruffs something
with the eight or nine, do
not overruff. Watch what
happens. Partner covers the
ten with the jack (or declarer
cashes the ace from hand) and
you play low both on this and
on declarer's second top heart.
Your queen and seven are
now both winners.

Layout
2

**You should not rush to
overruff the short trump hand
either.** Suppose you get the
chance to overruff dummy's
singleton jack of trumps
(diamonds). You must resist
the temptation. Look at the
full layout. You would just
score the king. By contrast,
by retaining K–9–x you
end up with two tricks—
remember, declarer cannot
finesse.

Layout
3

IMPORTANT POINT
*Overruffing with a
natural winner is
only likely to
be right if
your trump
intermediates are
poor, if partner
holds strong trumps
(for example, you
have K–x and partner
A–Q), or you need to
gain the lead quickly.*

Preparing for a trump promotion

Both sides vulnerable
Dealer South

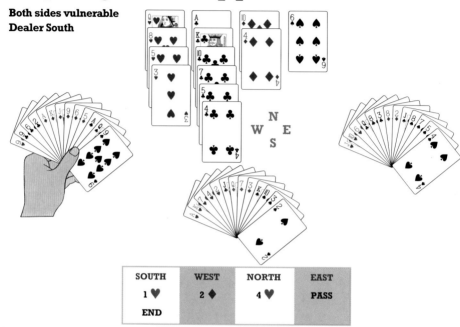

SOUTH	WEST	NORTH	EAST
1 ♥	2 ♦	4 ♥	PASS
END			

You, West, start with two top diamonds, on which East plays the eight and then the two. How should you continue?

What you know

With the doubleton diamond in dummy, partner would not encourage the suit holding Q–x–x. His high–low signal must mean a doubleton. If so, there is a good chance that he can overruff dummy, or come to a trump trick if dummy has to ruff high. The snag is that if you play a third diamond right away, declarer will ruff neither high nor low in dummy but discard the singleton spade instead.

The key plays

1. First you should cash the ♠A.
2. Only then do you play the third round of diamonds.
3. When dummy ruffs with the queen, partner has a sure trump trick.
4. If partner had the king of trumps, partner would overruff with it.
5. If partner had ♥J–x–x (no ten), dummy could ruff high but declarer would then have to guess whether you had J–x or a singleton trump.

IMPORTANT POINT *It is nearly always correct for the defenders to cash their side-suit winners before trying for a promotion,* *whether it is an uppercut or (as here) an overruff.*

Suit preference signals

If you win partner's spade lead with the ace, you may expect her to ruff the return. Therefore, you want to tell her what suit to lead next. If you want a high-ranking suit (diamonds, if hearts are trumps), return the ten. If you want the low-ranking suit (clubs, unless they are trumps), lead the two. If you are not sure what you want, lead the middling six.

Layout **1**

Layout **2**

If you read partner's lead of the three as a singleton, you want to play back the suit. Sadly, with only one low club for her to ruff, you cannot so easily give her a signal. The answer is to play your ace and king in reverse order (for instance, ace first), if you want a high-ranking suit back, and in normal order if you do not.

After you win the first trick with the ace and declarer ruffs your return of the four, the layout of the suit is clear to both defenders. There is no point, therefore, for a heart discard to say something about hearts. Instead, it should be suit-preference: the queen asks for the higher non-trump suit and the three for the lower-ranking suit.

Layout **3**

IMPORTANT POINT
Any signal that cannot logically show count or attitude should be a suit-preference signal. In deciding which suits it could ask for, you usually exclude the trump suit or some other strong opposing suit.

Glossary

advancer partner of one who overcalls or makes a takeout double.

balanced hand a hand with no singleton or void and at most one doubleton.

blockage and block when a player's high card in a short suit stops his side from running the suit, and to create such a position.

call a bid, double, redouble, or pass (no bid).

convention or conventional bid a bid with a special meaning, often something other than length in the denomination bid.

cue bid any bid in a suit shown by an opponent; also a bid to denote a specific holding in a suit, such as 1♥–(2♣)–3♣ or 1NT–3♥–4♣.

declarer the player who controls 26 cards, his own and dummy's.

denomination any of the four suits and no-trumps.

discard a card played from a suit different to the suit led, but not a trump, or (also throw or pitch) to play such a card.

doubleton a holding of exactly two cards in a suit.

duck the action of playing low when a high card is held, or to do so.

dummy the player with exposed cards controlled by declarer.

equals cards of equal value, usually in a sequence, such as K–Q.

finesse a positional play trying to win with a card that is not quite high, or to make such a play.

first-round control an ace or void.

fit partnership length in a suit sufficient to have it as trumps.

forcing bid a bid that requires partner to keep the bidding open.

game forcing requiring that the partnership bids to game.

game try a bid that invites partner to bid game with suitable values.

hold up withholding a stopper, or to withhold one

honor a ten, jack, queen, king, or ace.

interior (broken) sequence a holding in which the second- and third-highest cards are touching but the first is not (K–J–10).

invitational bid a bid that asks partner to bid higher with extra values.

jump a bid to a higher level than necessary, or to make such a bid.

lead the first play to a trick, or to make such a play.

limit bid a bid that shows a narrow range of values, such as 1NT–2NT.

negative a conventional response to deny specific values.

opening bid and opening bidder (or opener) the first positive bid in an auction and the player who makes such a bid.

opening lead and opening leader the lead to the first trick and the player who makes such a lead.

overcall a bid made after an opponent has opened, such as (1♣)–1♥.

overruff the play of a higher trump when another player has ruffed, or (also overtrump) to make such a play.

passed hand a player who passed (no bid) before anyone opened.

penalty double a double that partner is expected to leave in.

plain suit in a trump contract, the three suits that are not trumps.

preempt a jump bid normally based on shape and weakness to make life hard for the opposing side, or to make such a bid.

raise to bid or show the denomination that partner has just bid.

rebid a second or subsequent positive call (1♥–2♣–2♦).

response and responder a bid made by the partner of the opening bidder; the partner of the opening bidder.

reverse a sequence of two bids naming the lower suit first that makes it impossible to stop in two of the first suit (1♦–1♠–2♥).

ruff the play of a trump card on the lead of a plain suit, a trick won with such a card, and to play such a card.

running suit or solid suit a long suit with no losers (A–K–Q–J–10).

second-round control a king or singleton.

sequence usually three touching cards or two touching cards and a lower nearly touching card; also a series of bids.

signal the play of a card giving a predefined message to partner.

sign-off a bid that asks partner to pass (1♠–4NT–5♦–5♠).

singleton a holding of exactly one card in a suit.

spot card a card ranking below the jack.

stopper a high card that stops the opponents from running a suit.

support a holding in partner's suit that indicates a combined holding of, usually, at least eight cards, or to make a bid showing this.

switch or shift a lead of a new suit, or to make such a lead.

take-out double a double that asks partner to bid (1♦–double).

tenace two high cards of almost equal rank in a suit, such as A–Q.

touching of the rank just above or just below.

trump a card in the trump suit, or to ruff.

unbalanced hand a hand with a void, a singleton, or two doubletons.

unblock an action to avoid a blockage, or to take such an action.

underlead to lead low from, normally, an ace or a sequence.

uppercut a high ruff trying to promote a trump trick for partner.

void a holding of no cards in a suit.

Index

A

aces, unsupported 128
advancing 81, 95, 99
attitude signals 218
avoidance play 165, 203

B

balanced hands 26
    after 1NT 45
balancing 92, 95
Benjamin 77
bid suit leads 133
bidding process 12–13
Blackwood 69–70
blockage, to avoid 139
blocking opposing suit
    174

C

combining chances 162
competitive decisions
    114–117
continuations 28–29, 61,
    63, 68, 70
    defending 231
count, to rectify 209
count signals 219, 225
cue bids 68, 72, 83, 89,
    99, 117

D

deception 167
declarer 14
discard(s) 180
    defender's 240–244
    ruff and 199, 238, 239
    signals 243
discovery play 159

double(s): to continue
    with 104
    to handle 102–103
    initial 97
    lead-directing 110
    negative 83
    penalty 106–110,
    116
    protective 105
    standing 108–109
    takeout 96–101
drop, to play for 137
dropping high cards
    137, 148, 186
Drury 50
ducking 147, 216
dummy 14
    reversal 190
duplicate bridge 16–17

E

elimination play
    194–203, 206
elopement 205
entries: to attack 234
    to create 114
    to manage 145
    via a ruff 187
    trumps as 181
    to use effectively 164

F

felling high cards 148
finesse/finessing 137,
    138, 175
    against dummy 215
    ruffing 184
    two-way 160

five-card majors 23
five of a major 73
5NT inquiry 71
forcing 57, 117
    game 232
four-deal bridge 16–17
four- and five-level
    openings 32
4NT: inquiry 69–70
    opening 34
fourth highest 125, 230

G

gambling 3NT 33
game try 64, 66
guessing 161
    to avoid 194

H

holding up 168–169, 228
honors: to capture 227
    to cover 223
    to split 222

I

inferences 158
initial doubles 97
interior sequence lead
    124
inverted raises 37
invitational raise 45

J

jump overcalls 86–89
jump raises 37, 52
jump shift 43
    rebid 55

K
king–jack guesses 161

L
law of total tricks 113
lead(s): bid suit 133
    dangerous 233
    high 141–142
    to hold 183
    interior sequence 124
    low 140
    partner's suit 122–123
    sequence 120–121
    slam 134–136
    unbid suit 131–132
    unusual card 237
    up to weakness 236
lead-directing doubles 110
loser on loser 198
losers: to count 155
    to throw 240
losing trick count 19

M
matchpoints 17, 175
minor, response to 36
Morton's Fork 166
Multi 78

N
negative doubles 83
no-trump responses 67–68

O
one-level responses 40
1NT: opening 26
    overcall 84–85
    rebid 60–61
    response 39
    response to 45–47
opener's rebids 60, 62, 64, 65
opening bids 22–34
overcalls 79–81, 84, 86–91
    to handle 82–83, 85, 92–95
    to raise 80
overruff, to avoid 191, 247

P
partial elimination 200
partner's suit lead 122–123
partnerships 10
pass-out 13
passed hand responses 43, 50
penalty doubles 106–110, 116
penalty pass 100
penalty redoubles 111
play process 14
point count 18
points, to count 157
preemptive overcalls 88, 94–95
preempts 31, 32
preference 56, 67
probabilities 149

protecting 92, 105
protective doubles 105

R
raises: inverted 37
    invitational 45
    jump 37, 52
    strong 38
rebids:
    having doubled 101
    responder's 56–57, 59, 61, 63, 66
    same suit 58–59
redoubles 103, 111–112
reopening 92–93
responses 35–50
restricted choice 146
returns 230, 231
reverses 54
    responder's 42
rubber bridge 15
ruff/ruffing: to avoid 188, 189, 191
    to combat defensive 188
    cross 193
    defender's 245–249
    and discard 199, 238, 239
    down a high card 186
    in dummy 176
    entries 187
    finesse 184
    high 192
    long hand 182
    to make declarer 232
    to set up 177

Index

S

sacrificing 115–116
safety plays 143
sandwich seat 91
scissors coup 189
scoring: duplicate 16
 four-deal 16
 rubber 15
second hand low 220
second seat play
 150–151
shape, to count 156
short suit: leads 127
 to play 175
signals: attitude 218
 count 219, 225
 with discards 242
 suit-preference 229,
 249
slam: bidding 69–74
 leads 134–136
 try 74
SOS redoubles 112
splinter 52, 55
squeeze: automatic
 simple 207, 208
 double 210
 non-material 213
 to set up 209
 strip 211, 212
Standard American
 bidding 12
standing doubles
 108–109
Stayman 48
stopper, to knock out
 173
stripping the hand 202

strong club systems 75
strong raises 38
strong twos 29
suit(s): bad, to lead
 from 126
 evenly divided 197
 exit 197, 198, 201
 frozen 196
 non-touching 24
 not to play 153
 to play first 163, 173
 preference signals
 229, 249
 ranks 12
 risks of new 233
 second 53, 59, 67
 to set up 185
 short 127, 175
 touching 24
supporting partner 35,
 36, 51, 67, 101, 102

T

takeout doubles 96–105
tenace 165
 to exit in 201
 to get lead into 195
 to preserve 170
third hand high 214
three-level preempts 31
3NT: rebid 57, 65
 response 44
three-suited hands 25
touching cards 217
 to cover 224
transfers 49
tricks 19

where to win 154
trump(s): coup 204
 to draw 178
 to draw dummy's 235
 echo 226
 endplay 207
 as entries 181
 lead 129, 130
 to leave out 179
 promotion 246–248
two-club opening 27
two-level responses 41
2NT: opening 28
 overcall 90
 rebid 57, 62–63
 response 44
 response to 28
two-over-one system 76
two-suited hands 24
two-way finesses 160

U

unbid suit leads 131–132
uppercut 246

W

weak takeout 46
weak twos 30
winners: to keep 241,
 242
 to play for fast 172
winning quickly 172,
 221

What To Do Next?

You can learn only so much about bridge by studying a book or attending bridge lessons. You will want to go out and practice your newly acquired skills. If your partner or your friends already play then you can ask them where to go for a game. If you have attended a class, your teacher should be able to suggest a game suitable for you—perhaps fellow students will want to play. You could try putting up a notice at work inviting colleagues to join you for a lunchtime game. If none of these ideas works for you, then you will need external help.

You can look in the telephone directory for the name of your town/city followed by the words "bridge club." If you have access to the Internet, there are a variety of Web sites (listed on the next page) that can point you in the right direction. Do not worry that everyone in a club will be an expert. No matter what your standard, there will be others of a similar level to yourself. Another option is to play online bridge. Bridge can be an addictive game and, no matter the time of day or night, there will be people playing in an online game. Unless you live somewhere like Death Valley and literally are 100 miles from the nearest club, I would not recommend playing exclusively in online games. One of the great strengths of bridge is its social aspect and you will miss out if you never see your partner and opponents. Bridge attracts a wide variety of participants, the majority of whom will be kind and courteous and pleased to see you.

Most of the time, it is sensible to play with a partner of a similar standard or with similar aspirations to yourself. However, if you want to improve, you will probably need to play some of the time with a better or more experienced player. It can also help your game to play against opponents slightly stronger than yourself. This way you will witness firsthand what makes them successful and later use the winning strategies yourself.

Further Reading

Any book by Ron Klinger, Mike Lawrence, or Eddie Kantar is likely to be good. I can particularly recommend the following, which have largely self-explanatory titles:

Complete Book on Overcalls by Mike Lawrence
Guide to Better Card Play by Ron Klinger
Guide to Better Duplicate Bridge by Ron Klinger
Modern Bridge Defense by Eddie Kantar
Opening Leads by Mike Lawrence
Reese on Play by Terence Reese
Standard Bidding at Bridge with SAYC by Ellen Pomer/Ned Downey
The Two-Over-One System by Mike Lawrence (CD-rom)
Winning Contract Bridge [Complete] by Edgar Kaplan
Winning Declarer Play by Dorothy Hayden-Truscott

Useful Web Sites

www.acbl.org American Contract Bridge League—organization for bridge in the USA, Canada, Mexico, and Bermuda

www.baronbarclay.com U.S. supplier of bridge material

www.bridgeclublive.com online bridge club

www.bridgebase.com educational software and online bridge club

www.bridgeshop.com.au magazine and supplier of bridge material

www.bridgemagzine.co.uk magazine and supplier of bridge material

www.bridgeworld.com magazine

www.ecatsbridge.com great worldwide source of information

www.okbridge.com online bridge club

Credits

I want very much to thank **Maureen Dennison** for her editing work and **Peter Burrows** and **Danny Kleinman** for checking the manuscript. I would also like to mention that I referred to small parts of the text in my book **The Golden Rules for Rubber Bridge Players** published by Cassell.

Thanks also to the Young Chelsea Bridge Club (www.ycbc.co.uk) for their support in producing images for this publication.

Image on page 7 © CORBIS.